THE ZIMZUM OF LOVE

A New Way of Understanding Marriage

ROB BELL AND
KRISTEN BELL

WILLIAM
COLLINS

William Collins
An imprint of HarperCollins*Publishers*
1 London Bridge Street
London
SE1 9GF

WilliamCollinsBooks.com

First published in Great Britain in 2014 by William Collins
This paperback edition published in Great Britain in 2016 by William Collins

19 18 17 16

10 9 8 7 6 5 4 3 2 1

Designed by Terry McGrath
Illustrations by John Stevens
Photograph on page 120 by Carolyn Baas

A catalogue record for this book is available from the British Library

ISBN 978-0-00-758208-2

Printed and bound in Great Britain by Clays Ltd, St Ives plc

THE ZIMZUM OF LOVE

CONTENTS

PREFACE

A while ago we came across an idea about the origins of the universe that made us think of marriage. We weren't aware that anyone had connected this idea with being married, and it got us thinking. The more we talked about it, the more this idea evolved into a new way of understanding marriage. We found ourselves thinking *we should write a book about this*.

So for a year and a half now, we wake up in the morning and make breakfast for our kids and take them to school, and then we sit side by side at a desk, doing our best to give language to this new way of understanding marriage.

There are, of course, lots of books on marriage. Practical books, inspiring books, books that can give you all sorts of advice and steps and techniques for facing and dealing with the challenges of marriage, from communicating better to handling money to sex to the division of household tasks.

This book, however, is about the deeper mysteries of marriage. How is it that the same relationship can be capable of producing so much joy *and* so much pain? How is it that the slightest thoughts and actions can so significantly change the space between two people? How is it that the space between two people can be so unique that it exists nowhere else in the universe? How is it that flawed, fragile, flesh-and-blood human beings can relate to each other in such a way that they show each other the divine?

Something powerful and profound happens in marriage—something involving energy, love, and the deepest forces of the universe. We believe that you can grow in your awareness of these realities, learning how to better see what's going on in the space between you, how it works, and how the love can flow all the more freely between you.

To that end, we've included discussion questions at the end of this book as well as endnotes with commentary to help you explore these deeper mysteries together.

It's our hope that this new way helps you better understand and enjoy this mysterious, extraordinary, difficult, beautiful, frustrating, complicated gift called marriage.

THE ZIMZUM OF LOVE

CHAPTER 1

WHAT'S A ZIMZUM?

We want to give you a new way of understanding marriage.

It's called the *zimzum of love,* and we explain it with stick figure drawings.

At first, it's just you.

Your life is mostly about you. Your friends and your work and your schedule and your interests and your goals and your thoughts and all the rest of what makes your life *your life.*

Your center of gravity extends roughly as far as you.

But then you meet someone—or you've known someone
for a while—and that person has their own life, with their
own center of gravity, and your heart begins to shift
toward them.

You find yourself thinking about them, drawn to them.
When you're not with them, you miss them, you ache for
them, your phone rings and when you see that it's them
you feel a surge of electricity through your body.

You talk for hours. You start arranging your life so that
you can spend as much time as possible with them as
your lives become increasingly intertwined.

As you become familiar with what moves and drives and inspires them, their well-being begins to matter to you more than your own. You find yourself making sacrifices for them,

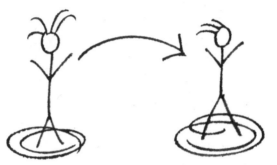

while they're doing the same for you.

It's here that you become aware of a subterranean shift, a tectonic slide in your heart, one that alters the course of your life:

Your center of gravity *expands*.

You are in new territory.

Before, it was just you.

Now, it's you—and this other person.

Before, there was one.

Now, there are two.

As you intentionally create space for this person in your life and they create space in their life for you, this movement creates *space between you*—space that has an energetic flow to it.

This flow in the space between you is like an energy field or an electrical current. It's the draw, the pull, the magnetic attraction that leads you to give yourself to this person in a way you don't give yourself to anyone else on the planet.

It's a vibrant, pulsing, humming flow that stirs your heart and causes your soul to soar. You talk about falling in love because of the feeling of weightlessness it evokes; you speak of finding your other half because of those moments when your boundaries feel porous, like you don't know where you end and they begin. You speak of being swept away, like you're caught up in something bigger than the both of you, like you're flying, the intoxicating attraction you feel toward another human being taking you both somewhere new and thrilling.

And then there's us, standing in our kitchen arguing about something one of us said about the microwave.

K: It was me. I made a comment—

R: —that made no sense.

K: And then he wouldn't drop it.

R: I couldn't figure out what she was talking about.

K: And so he got butt-headed about it.

R: Just explain what you meant.

K: Just drop it. Let it go. Relax.

R: So you're saying you didn't mean it?

K: I'm saying it's not worth discussing.

R: Then why did you say it?

We're going round and round having the dumbest discussion in which neither of us is actually listening to the other and it's getting more and more ridiculous because we're making less and less sense—and then our older son, who's been sitting there the entire time witnessing this train wreck of a conversation, finally says,

K: With his head in his hands,

Will you two stop it? You're driving me crazy!

(We're laughing as we write this.)

There are moments in marriage when you realize that you're brushing up against our deepest experiences of what it means to be human, when you become aware that some of the most profound truths of the universe are lying next to you in bed, moments that illuminate our most innate and mysterious longings for grace and connection and vitality.

And then there are *other* moments, when lofty talk about two becoming one and *I found my other half* seems delusional, when you wonder, *Who is this crazy person and why in the world did I ever want to be married to them?*

Marriage.

You find someone—or they find you (that's part of the mystery, isn't it?)—and out of seven billion people on the planet, you decide to say yes *to just one of them,* till death do you part.

There is something about marriage—something about the potential, the promise, and the possibilities of creating a life together—something so powerful and compelling and alluring that despite all the pain marriage has caused over the years, people are still looking for that one person—and still getting married.

Still standing on beaches staring into each other's eyes for engagement photos, still registering for matching bath towels, still trying to figure out whether or not the groomsmen should wear the cummerbunds, because, after all, they're included in the rental.

K: The dating site match.com gets around seventeen million unique visitors *a month.* Seventeen million people a month holding out hope that *that* person is out there.

There's all sorts of speculation about exactly how many marriages don't last—the general consensus being *quite a few*—but statistics are beside the point because we've all seen marriages unravel around us—neighbors, co-workers, parents of our kids' friends—people taking off wedding rings, selling houses, working out joint custody arrangements.

Divorce is like a death, only the other person is still alive.

Some say that the enduring draw of marriage is rooted in cultural conditioning. And they have a point. Our daughter was watching a movie recently about a princess who was waiting for her prince to rescue her so that they could live happily ever.

And she's *four* (our daughter, not the princess).

Others say that our ongoing propensity to keep getting hitched is simply biology in its more advanced and organized forms, that we're hardwired to find someone to make more someones with and so marriage is simply a social construct we've created to propagate our species.

R: Two words about that: *throw pillows.*

K: Throw pillows?

R: Dudes learning to properly arrange throw pillows on the couch because *that's how she likes it.*

K: What do you mean by that?

R: There's a direct connection between primal mating impulses rooted in biological survival instincts and the intentional organizing of decorative cushions.

K: In other words, our species has an astonishing ability to adapt.

And then there's the Jagger Theory (as in, Mick), which states in a very straightforward manner that monogamy isn't our natural inclination so why do we keep torturing ourselves with this outdated and antiquated custom that shackles two people to the constricting notion that they must remain exclusively and faithfully committed to each other with no other experiences of a similar sort until one of them is left standing over the grave of the other?

That question leads to another question, one many people have about marriage: Has any institution/idea/arrangement caused so many people so much agony? Is there a greater ache than giving your heart—not to mention your life—to someone, only to have it collapse and fall apart on you?

Some say the expectations are the problem. If people just lived together in peace and harmony without all the legal obligations and wedding rings and assumptions that come from having a public ceremony in front of your friends and family with cake and an eighties cover band, then there would be a lot less heartache if things don't work out. But sharing your life with someone—whatever that looks like—always involves challenges, and if you part ways, that kind of pain is always heartbreaking.

But whether there's a ceremony or a ring or a legal document or not, whether it's biology or cultural conditioning or simply pressure from the relatives, there is an enduring human longing to share our life with someone.

||||||||||||||||||||

For us, it started in a pickup truck.

It was an early eighties Mazda pickup with a cab on the back and black stripes down the side.

R: I bought it from my neighbor, Dr. Dull.

K: It had a cassette player bolted under the dashboard with the smallest speakers you've ever seen.

R: That's what you remember about that truck—its tiny speakers?

K: What I remember most are the butterflies I had in my stomach the first time I got into that truck. I was living in Arizona at the time and Rob was living in Los Angeles, and when I was accepted into a master's program at USC, I called him and asked if he would help me find a place to live.

R: Which sounded a little suspicious to me because it was January and her program didn't start until June.

K: I could say I was just planning ahead—but the truth is, I wanted to know whether this was something more than a friendship.

R: So as I pulled up to "Arrivals" at the airport, I had the strong sense that there was something else going on here. I thought it was better just to get it out in the open, and so when she got in the truck I asked her, "What percentage of your visit is actually to look for a place to live?" She smiled and said, "Well, it makes a great excuse." I will never forget the BOOM!!! that went off in my heart when she said that.

K: Maybe we should back up for a moment. I grew up in Arizona, Rob grew up in Michigan, and we met on a tennis court our freshman year at Wheaton College.

R: To be honest, I knew who she was before we met on that tennis court. During freshmen orientation they gave us a book called *Who's New,* which was filled with pictures of incoming freshmen. My friends and I spent hours poring over that book. One of those first days of college, sitting in my room in Traber dorm, I came across Kristen's picture. Wow, I thought. I should meet her, so that we could, um, study together.

K: I don't remember Rob studying much, but I do remember once during that freshman year having a conversation with him about cactus. He was fascinated with cactus and couldn't imagine that I came from a place where we had a large cactus in our yard.

R: Fascinated with cactus? (Cacti?) Really? That may be the lamest excuse I've ever heard for chatting up a girl. I suddenly developed an interest in cactus? Did I know how pathetic that must have sounded at the time?

K: Apparently it worked because that summer I sent him a letter (remember those?) with a photo of me standing next to a very large cactus.

R: I remember that photo. And I remember those letters. Our friendship was like that for four years—inside jokes, letters back and forth, having a meal together every now and then, going out as a group with my friends and her friends.

K: I'd go watch Rob's band perform. He had written one song in particular that moved me. The fact that he'd written those lyrics made me wonder what else was in there.

All of which brings us to graduation.

K: I was headed home to work in Arizona.

R: And I was moving to California, which meant driving through Arizona. In one of the first conversations Kristen and I ever had, we talked about waterskiing, and she said that her family had a MasterCraft, which to me was about the greatest boat a person could own, so I said, "Well, I ought to stop by sometime and we could go waterskiing."

K: Which I thought would never actually happen.
But then at graduation he reminded me of that
conversation four years earlier, and he said, "Can
I stop by at the end of the summer so we can go
waterskiing?" A few months later he showed up at my
parents' house and stayed for several days. When he
left, I hoped I would see him again. But I had no idea
how that would work.

R: And so I continued on to L.A.

K: And I continued on with my life.

R: And I moved in with my eighty-two-year-old
grandmother to take care of her while I went to
seminary.

K: And then I got the early acceptance letter from USC,
and I called him to tell him I'd be moving to L.A.—and
the next thing I knew I was getting in that truck and
saying, "It makes a great excuse."

R: Which was a great line, by the way. Classic.

K: Thank you. But I think there's an important point to
make to here. I knew what I was getting into, and I'm
not just talking about the truck. I already knew his
friends, his family; I'd seen him in all kinds of different
situations—there weren't any surprises. I was ready to
see whether this was headed somewhere.

R: Which it was. Specifically, to my grandma's apartment.
How killer is that? Me and this hot woman from the

desert and my grandma, chillin' on the green polyester couch with the paisley stitching.

You can be friends with someone, sometimes even for years, with a tremendous amount of respect and friendship and history between you, but when that spark ignites, everything changes.

Several months later we were living in the same city, shortly after that we were engaged, nine months later we were married, and twenty years later we're still exploring the endless depths of whatever it is that began when Kristen got in that truck and we drove off together.

||||||||||||||||||||||

You find each other, your centers of gravity expand as your lives become more and more entwined. You create space for this other person to thrive

while they're doing the same for you.

This creates a flow of energy in the space between you.

This energy field is at the heart of marriage. It flows in the space between you, space that exists nowhere else in the universe.

You can become more familiar with how this energy field works.

You can develop language between you to identify what's happening in the space between you.

You can sharpen your abilities to assess it.

You can act in certain ways to increase the flow.

You can identify what's blocking the flow, and then you can overcome those barriers.

Years into your marriage, you can continue to intensify this energetic flow between you.

It is risky to give yourself to another. There are no guarantees, and there are lots of ways for it to fall apart and break your heart. *But the upside is infinite.*

There is a mysterious, indescribable, complex exchange that can happen in the space between you, filling you with joy, confirming your intuition that marriage is not only good for you, but good for the world. Marriage has the uniquely powerful capacity to transform you both into more loving and generous and courageous and compassionate people. Marriage—gay and straight—is a gift to the world because the world needs more—not less—love, fidelity, commitment, devotion, and sacrifice.

We're for marriage, and we want to give you a new way of understanding marriage.

We call this way the *zimzum of love.*

Which of course raises the question:
What's a zimzum?

||||||||||||||||||||||

K: Rob loves words. I realize that may sound strange, but
he loves finding new words and odd phrases and then
using them around the house, repeating them and
thinking they're hilarious. And the more random the
better, like *catty wompus* or *rusty Kleenex.*

R: Or *Engelbert Humperdinck—*

K: —as I was saying . . .

R: Or *unpidgeonholeable—*

K: Yes?

R: —or *fog index* or *history of fishes* . . .

K: In the last page of endnotes in his book *What We
Talk About When We Talk About God* Rob gives a list
of words and phrases and names for apparently no
reason other than sheer enjoyment.

R: Like the word *cummerbund.*

K: Cummerbund?

R: The thing some men for unknown reasons choose to wear around their midsections at weddings. It's a Persian word, from the word *kamar,* which means waist—it's actually a *kamar band.*

K: I rest my case. Which is why it didn't surprise me when he started using the word *zimzum.*

R: *Zimzum* (originally *tzimtzum*) is a Hebrew word used in the rabbinic tradition to talk about the creation of the world—not in a scientific way but more like something somewhere between poetry and metaphysical speculation. Followers of this tradition began with the assumption that before there was anything, there was only God. The divine, they believed, was all that was. For something to exist other than God, then, God had to create space that *wasn't* God. A bit esoteric, but stay with me. Their contention was that for something to exist that wasn't God, God had to contract or withdraw from a certain space so that something else, something other than God, could exist and thrive in that space. And the word they used for this divine contraction is *zimzum.* God *zimzums,* so that everything we know to be everything can exist and thrive.

We loved this word *zimzum,* and we were struck with how well it describes what happens when you're married. The more we talked about it, the more we found ourselves bending and stretching this word, making it our own.

You meet this person, you fall in love, and you *zimzum*— creating space for them to thrive while they're doing the same for you. This zimzuming unleashes energy and creates space that didn't exist before, generating the flow that is the lifeblood of marriage.

To illustrate how this flow works, we'll explore four aspects of this space, space that is **responsive, dynamic, exclusive,** and **sacred.**

CHAPTER 2

RESPONSIVE

The space between you is extremely **responsive.**

We've drawn this image for responsive as a large, bold arrow toward the other person because everything you do and everything you are affects the flow between the two of you. It's like a finely tuned radar, or the needle on a record player, the slightest notes and sounds amplified along with every bit of dust or the smallest scratch.

People often aren't aware of just how responsive the space between them is. It matters what you say, it matters what you do, it matters how you think about this other person, it matters how you think about yourself. All of it, good and bad, shapes the flow between you.

To keep this energy field full of life and vitality, you intentionally act for their well-being. This movement is the foundation of your life together. It's what everything rests on. It's the engine, the catalyst, the energy that keeps the space between you humming. It's what you return to again and again.

The arrow moves from you to them while another comes back to you. That's how the flow starts, that's how it's sustained, and that's how you get it going again when it's blocked. You're looking out for their best while they're looking out for yours.

K: I don't really enjoy talking on the phone. I'll blame it on being an introvert. I much prefer face-to-face conversations. Transitions like ending a phone call are hard for me, and that combined with an overdeveloped sense of empathy can leave me feeling stuck for a painfully long time. Once in a while I'll have to return a difficult call—something socially awkward or a call in which I have to say *no* to somebody—and it will haunt me all day. I tell you this because one day Rob brought home a jacket he'd just bought.

R: I remember that jacket. I loved that jacket. The salesman loved that jacket. Other people in the store loved that jacket.

K: And he put it on for me, and I immediately said *No way*.

R: She did. Not the slightest doubt. She just shut that jacket down.

K: It had a weird curve in the stitching on the back that just wasn't right. It looked like a woman's jacket.

R: You're killing me right now.

K: No, I was saving you.

R: I've learned over time to trust her instincts; so I was fine taking it back. Except for one thing: I couldn't face the salesman. He had been so excited about that jacket. This pains me to admit, but I couldn't take that jacket back because I couldn't face that salesman. How pathetic is that? So in the heat of the moment, desperate, I offered Kristen a deal.

K: Actually, *I* offered the deal: I'll take back the jacket for you if you'll do a hundred awkward phone calls for me.

R: I took that deal so fast. I still have something like ninety-six to go.

We realize this story is ridiculous.

K: I would have taken that jacket back for him without THE DEAL.

R: And I'll make an awkward phone call for her anytime.

But we tell this story because there's a back and forth, a give and take that happens when you zimzum.

You ask, *What do you want? What do you need?*
They tell you.
They ask you the same questions.
You answer.
They listen.
You talk about it.
You do things for each other.

You make deals, and then you laugh about how absurd it is to make deals because you would have done it anyway.

The arrows take you toward each other, creating a sense of momentum as the energy circulates in the space between you.

K: I was traveling in Europe a number of years ago and spent a few days with a newly married couple from the States who had moved there to work together. At one point I was having a meal with the wife and asked her what she saw herself doing in five years. I was surprised with her response, because she talked about living on a different continent, pursuing a degree in a field totally unrelated to the work they were currently doing. Because I had interacted with her husband before this and had heard some of his hopes and plans, I had the growing impression that they hadn't talked about any of this with each other. They seemed to have lost the glue, the spark, the fire that brought them together in the first place, and they were headed in different directions.

To act, you first have to know.

You have to know what it looks like for them to thrive; you have to be aware of their goals and dreams; you have to know what they want and what they need and what makes them feel secure and what makes them happy and fulfilled.

It's amazing how much can change between you when you ask, *What do you need?*

R: People used to hold up signs at football games that read "JOHN 3:16"—remember those? (The person holding the sign up was usually sitting next to the dude in the rainbow wig.) Those signs were referring to a verse in the Bible about how God loves the world so much that God sent God's son. The big word in that verse is, of course, *that*. Divine love is the kind of love *that* does something.

K: It's one thing to be *in* love; it's another to act *because of* love. Love is a noun—a feeling you *have*—and it's also a verb, something you *do*.

The space between you is highly responsive because it's *generative* space—whatever you put into it multiplies exponentially.

Have you ever had an argument or a fight or an epic blowup and then later, when the dust settled and you talked about it, you realized that the whole thing started with something small?

An off-handed comment, a subtle slight, an expectation that wasn't met, a job around the house that you kept avoiding—it wasn't that big of a deal, but it grew and expanded and gained a head of steam as it completely changed the space between you. This is what happens in a generative space—things are magnified beyond their actual size.

One moment your marriage is pure joy, and the next sheer misery, the beautiful friendship and ease you had between you gone; you don't even want to be in the same room.

This is why marriage can be so difficult *and* so great: the space that multiplies and magnifies any negativity between you also multiplies and magnifies the generous and kind things you do for each other.

R: We were in a surf shop, and I noticed the tide watch the guy behind the counter was wearing. (A tide watch tells you how high or low the water is, which affects when the waves are best for surfing.) Kristen apparently noticed me noticing his watch, because a few weeks later she gave me the same watch. I've been wearing it for years, and to this day, when I check the time, I'm struck by how often I think of her. It's just a watch. But after twenty years together, it's way more than just a watch—it's a sign, a symbol, a reminder that this woman is looking out for me.

This generative space responds to whatever you put into it, magnifying the good things you do for each other as well as the negative things that echo between you. This is true for *whatever* you bring to the space, including the things that you aren't aware of.

K: In the summer of 2004 Rob was speaking in California, and the boys and I joined him to make a family vacation out of it. One night on that trip he went to bed early without saying good night.

R: I was exhausted, and I was trying to fall asleep but I couldn't because the television in the other room was so loud. Kristen was watching Letterman, and it sounded like she was turning the volume up.

K: Which I was. I was angry. But it actually went much deeper than that.

R: I was in that half-awake/half-sleep state, and Renée Zellweger was Dave's guest and all I could think was, "Renée, please stop talking so loud."

K: I was angry because he had energy for all of these other people but not for me. He had been distant for some time, and I wondered whether he still loved me. I thought, *Maybe this is just how it is when you've been married for a while.*

R: I didn't have anything to give. I had been working too hard for too long, pushing myself beyond my limits.

K: It was hard for me to start the conversation because I wondered whether my fears were true—that his love for me had faded. But the next day when we started talking, it became clear that it had nothing to do with how he felt about *me.*

R: The real reason for our disconnection wasn't my lack of love for Kristen—it was my emotional health. I was cooked, burned out, empty, exhausted, running on fumes, and up until that conversation I hadn't been aware of how it was affecting both of us.

Your emotional health matters.

It matters when you meet someone, it matters when you're committing to spend the rest of your life with that person, and it matters when you've been together for one or seven or twenty years. Whatever history and baggage and issues you bring to your marriage, they now belong to both of you because when you get married, whatever is *yours* is now *ours*.

We bring our entire selves to the space between us.

The arrow leaves you and extends to them—that's how the flow is sustained. Whatever it is—unresolved issues with your family of origin, addictions, struggles, emotional scars, wounds from past relationships, regrets, destructive habits, unhealthy patterns of reaction or avoidance—it's all there in the shared space between you.

You cannot keep your issues to yourself. *The space is too responsive.* It's like a motion sensor, picking up the most subtle movements. You can't hide anything, even if you think you're hiding it.

It's an illusion that whatever it is, "it doesn't affect the marriage," or "what they don't know won't hurt them," or "it's not a big deal."

It does, it will, and it is.

You're intentional about your own health because your marriage will only be as healthy as the least healthy one of you.

As counterintuitive as it may seem, taking care of *yourself* is one of the best gifts you can give the person you are married to. This includes exercising, eating well, getting enough sleep, engaging in regular practices that feed your soul—these are all essential to giving your best to the person you love.

This isn't about perfection; it's about the direction you're headed in, the trajectory you're on, both of you—and the two of you together—refusing to settle, pursuing the best possible life together.

Pain and discomfort and the gnawing sense that things could be better are your friends. They wake you up, they stir you to action, they motivate you to get help. This may mean initiating difficult conversations, finding help in a book or class or retreat, or seeing a therapist or doctor or spiritual director.

Sometimes a disruption is the best thing for the space between you.

R: That trip to California was a disruption for me. When we returned, I began to uncover with a counselor the reasons why I had been pushing myself so hard. It was life changing.

Sometimes the problem is you.

You brought something to the space that you haven't dealt with, and it's affecting you both. Until you deal with it, it will continue to have a negative effect on the flow between you. The space, however, is highly responsive, and it's surprising how even the smallest steps toward health can significantly change things.

ııllıllıllıllıllıllıllıll

You zimzum, they zimzum, you know they'd do anything for you, you talk about what makes each of you thrive, the arrows go back and forth—that's what creates the energetic flow between you.

But then there are the times when the arrows don't feel equal. Times when you feel like you're doing your part, but they aren't doing theirs. In those moments it's easy to become resentful, keeping track of who's doing what, clutching your scorecard.

You know the scorecard, right?

The scorecard is how we keep track of how much we're giving and how much they're giving and who's sacrificing more and who's carrying more of the weight and who's got the lighter load and who's taken on more of the responsibility so that the other can pursue their goals and who's working harder at the relationship and who owes more and who's turn it is to empty the dishwasher. The scorecard is at the heart of an extraordinary number of fights; it lurks in the shadows of lots of heated discussions, and if it's not addressed and is left unchecked, it can poison the space between you.

The scorecard is rooted in resentment, *and the space between you is highly responsive to resentment.* Even the slightest tremors of bitterness can block the flow of love.

The scorecard makes you feel alone. It feels like they aren't looking out for you. And if they aren't, then you need to look out for yourself. There's a sinking feeling that comes from believing you're on your own.

The scorecard makes you feel entitled—*I'm the one making the money, I'm the one watching the kids all day, I'm the one looking after the house.* You find yourself arguing your case for why you've racked up more points.

R: Like when the dude is out with his friends and he says *he has the night off.* Really? Like the rest of the time—*namely, when he's home*—he's working, earning points?

K: Or when he does something kind or generous and she says *that's the least he can do*—implying that she is owed and therefore entitled.

The scorecard makes you want to disengage and step back and withdraw, waiting for them to make the first move because, after all, *Why should I keep giving if they aren't?*

You know you've got a scorecard when you find yourself nagging, feeling resentful, complaining, and being critical—all driven by the desire to arouse some sort of response from them.

The scorecard is like a vortex, sucking you both in, deeper and deeper—each of you racking up points, the tension building, fine tuning your case as you go for why you're the one who's right, who's carrying more, who's more committed, who's got more invested.

This vortex is lethal because it's rooted in fear—fear that we're on our own, that we're not going to be taken care of, that we're not going to get what we need. This fear causes us to clutch and cling all the more tightly to ourselves, looking out for our needs, protecting ourselves.

In order to get rid of the scorecard, you have to choose to act in love instead of in fear. There's a reason why this works, and it's based on the way our brains function.

Your brain has a number of different parts. One part reacts with lightning speed when it senses that you're vulnerable or under attack. This is the seat of anger in your brain; it's not rational, and its purpose is to protect you. When it senses a threat, it immediately decides whether to fight or flee. Without it, we wouldn't have survived as a species.

This is why so many scorecard fights are irrational—whatever the fear is, it has activated the part of the brain that *isn't rational.*

We react,
we grow more fearful,
we're easily angered,
our thoughts spiral out of control.

There are, obviously, other parts of your brain that are far more advanced. One part is the seat of your logical thinking; it's where you compare data and analyze options and make reasoned decisions. Another part of your brain is the seat of love and empathy and compassion.

Here's why it's so important to act in love, not in fear: **The primitive, protective, fearful, survival part of your brain can't run at the same time as the other rational, loving parts.**

Why does this matter for the scorecard?
Because when you are resentful or angry, the most powerful thing you can do is to act in love and

compassion. This literally shuts off the part of your brain that keeps you in the vortex.

To get rid of your scorecard, someone has to move toward the other first.

The arrow goes from you to them because one of you has to move toward the other in love. Not with accusations, and not in fear, and not with a summary of who has what points. One of you has to break the cycle. One of you has to tear up your scorecard first.

Sometimes this is as straightforward as sitting down and looking the other person in the eyes and saying

I am for you.
I've got your back.
I am committed to your best.
Help me understand things from your perspective.
What can we do together to change things?

When one person moves toward the other, the other is freed to respond in love. Something powerful happens when you remind each other that you are *for* each other. It reconnects you to your intentions. It reminds you of your original zimzum. It creates a foundation for your conversation. It eases your fears and allows you to speak rationally about how you're going to work it out, what needs to change, and the practical steps you're going to take to make change happen.

There is a science to the responsive space between you. Brains and bodies and hearts and minds—you bring all of you to the space, and when you move toward the other in love, you are activating powerful forces between you.

||||||||||||||||||||||

One arrow moves from you to them, another from them back to you. You talk about what you each need and want. You calm each other's fears. You do this because you love each other.

And love, if it's going to last, always involves sacrifice.

There's **spark kind of love.** That's the desire, the passion, the romance, the feeling like your heart has been hijacked. It's what happens when someone consumes your thoughts.

It's that rush of adrenaline and dopamine that makes a person feel like they're flying, the same chemicals firing in the brain that cocaine activates. Researchers have found that physiologically the body can keep up that intensity for only six to nine months. If that's all that's going on between you, eventually the high wears off and the passion is gone and you realize that there wasn't much more to the relationship.

Spark is thrilling, but sometimes spark is simply infatuation, and it fades. It comes on strong, it's intense and all-consuming, but it can't be sustained.

R: It burns bright and hot but then fizzles out.

Spark is absolutely necessary—but if you have only spark with another person, it's only a matter of time before they're driving you crazy. Or you're bored.

Then there's **substance kind of love.** Substance includes the character and integrity and qualities that you admire in this person. Substance involves shared values, what you have in common. Substance is when you realize, *This is my best friend.* Spark comes and goes, but substance is always there. Substance endures.

And then there's **sacrifice kind of love.** Sacrifice is when it costs you something to love this person, and it's a price you gladly pay.

When spark and substance come together, the result is electric. People talk about falling in love with their soul mate. But if it's going to endure, if the love is going to last and you're going to create a life together, there will inevitably be times when you have to make sacrifices.

K: We're always moved by love that makes sacrifices.

R: Like the final episode of the final season of the television show *Friday Night Lights* when Tami gets a job offer from a college in Philadelphia. When she tells her husband, the Coach, he won't even discuss it.

K: I sense I should give a spoiler warning.

R: It's about this couple in a small town in Texas, and he's the high school football coach and she's the principal of the school and she gets a job offer from a college in Philadelphia, which means he would have to leave his job and he is, after all, a High School Football Coach in Texas and yet she wants the job and the tension keeps building and you the viewer can't imagine them *not* living in Texas and him *not* being the Coach and yet you're also rooting for her.

K: Don't leave us hanging here.

R: And then there's that moment when he stops at the mall on the way to the state championship game because he knows she's there with their daughter and he finds her and she's surprised and wonders why he isn't on his way to the game and he says that he wants her to take the job and he wants her to take him with her to Philadelphia—and it's just so moving.

K: It's especially moving because it's rare. Most of the love stories we see are about two people finally confessing their love for each other, usually in the last scene and usually when it's raining or one of them has just run through an airport to stop the other one from getting on a plane. We're left to assume that this was the one big obstacle in their way and now they will live happily ever after. But that's just the beginning.

R: Which is the power of a scene like this one in *Friday Night Lights*. It isn't about the fireworks of that falling-in-love moment at the beginning. Instead, it's about a couple working it out in everyday life with all of the costs and rewards and struggles and sacrifice that it takes.

In the ancient wisdom of the Christian tradition, love always leads to sacrifice. **And nothing transforms the space between you more than sacrifice.**

For many people, sacrifice, especially in marriage, is a negative. It's about what you give up. It's about what you don't get to do. It's about what you miss out on because you put the other person first. It may be moving to a city that you don't want to move to for *their* job, or picking up more responsibility around the house because *they're* not feeling well, or spending money on something for *them* when there are all kinds of things you would have loved to spend that money on.

The problem with this misunderstanding of sacrifice is that it makes marriage all about you.

You *can* live for yourself.

You can live with a center of gravity as wide and deep as your own needs and interests and desires. You can be *self*-centered. In doing this, your life will be as big as you.

Or, you can love this person you're married to in such a way that they know without a shadow of a doubt that you'd lay down your life for them.

The arrows move from you and head toward the other because sacrifice is the most powerful thing you can do for the space between you. One of you stretches for one season and then the other for another season; you each give and you each make sacrifices—it's all part of marriage. **If you keep this up over time—this back and forth, this give and take—you eventually begin to lose track of who's been giving and sacrificing more. And the scorecard starts to disappear.**

There's a great line from a collection of Hebrew poems in the Bible called Song of Songs:

I am my beloved's and my beloved is mine.

Does he belong to her or does she belong to him? Which is it?

The answer is *Yes*. Both are true.

Each person has given first, served first, put the other first, *first*. They have each given themselves to the other in such a way that two things are happening at the same time.

When you are both intentional about moving toward the other in love, over time you build up tremendous reserves of love and grace and goodwill. Love—with spark and substance and sacrifice all together—is a cumulative phenomenon. It builds on itself, it gains a head of steam, it grows in depth and breadth and intensity. This propels you into an entirely different way of relating to each other—another kind of life altogether.

||||||||||||||||||||||

The language we use reveals what we believe is possible. Take the phrase *staying together.* Staying together is significant, but if that's the point—that is, *not breaking up*—then that may be all you have. Or the phrase *as good as it gets,* which usually means *we can't do any better* or *we've given up.*

The truth is that you can change things, because the space between you *responds* to your actions and intentions.

Everything that matters takes tremendous intention and will and energy. This includes marriage. New possibilities are created when you decide you are going to do something and then you give yourself to it and you don't give up.

You can take steps to be more healthy.
You can throw away your scorecard.
You can give yourself to their well-being.

K: You can take the jacket back.

R: You can return those calls.

You can make sacrifices.

You can be propelled into an entirely different mode of relating.

Out of the billions of people on the planet, you fell in love with this one person. You may have had spark with other people along the way, or you may have friends with whom you share a lot of common substance or someone you would do anything for, but in this one particular person, all these loves came together.

And so you took a leap. You exchanged vows, you committed to each other, you set out to make a life together. You had no guarantees, you knew it was a risk, but something within you told you that *this is where life is*—with this person.

R: If you aren't clear about what you want, life will just happen to you. Survival is one thing, *thrival* is another.

K: I think you just made that word up.

R: I did. It's a good one. *Thrival.*

CHAPTER 3
DYNAMIC

The space between you is **responsive,** and it's also **dynamic.**

We've drawn dynamic as a series of waves because life never stops changing. Whether events or circumstances are changing or the person you're married to is changing, it's inevitable that these changes will affect the space between you.

In the same way that the space is *responsive* to whatever you bring to it, the dynamic nature of life will affect the space positively or negatively.

You can learn to navigate this dynamic space together. Whether it's financial stress or success in work or health issues or personal growth or challenges in raising kids— **everything that comes your way can be an opportunity for the love to flow more freely between you.**

There are *seasons* in marriage: When you first get together and you're totally absorbed in each other is a very different season from the one when you're both starting new jobs or when your first kid goes off to school or when you're remodeling a house or your work involves long hours or extended travel—which is a very different season from the one when you're dealing with the illness of a parent or all your kids move out of the house or your business is faltering or one of you is struggling with depression or the other is recovering from surgery.

K: Or when we started a church, and it was so all-consuming that even when we weren't working we were talking about working.

R: Or when we had our first baby and we were both sleep deprived.

K: Or when you were on a speaking tour and I was home with three kids in the middle of a dark, icy winter.

R: And I was calling home to tell you about all the people I was meeting and experiences I was having and you were quiet on the other end of the line.

K: And I was trying to be happy for you but what I was really feeling was resentment.

R: And I was wondering from two thousand miles away whether that subdued tone in your voice was actually resentment and when I got home you weren't going to burst out of the front door and rush to greet me and throw your arms around me and welcome me home but instead you'd hand me a child with a loaded diaper and say, *Your turn.*

Sometimes, it's obvious when one season ends and another starts. Other times, the transition is far more subtle and can easily go unnoticed. Some seasons happen because of choices you make; others arrive unexpectedly and uninvited. Some seasons come and go quickly; others feel like they drag on and on.

Some seasons are particularly difficult, and it's all you can do to hang in there, reminding yourself that it's a season, and seasons come and go, and it's not always going to be like this.

However long or short or difficult or easy a season is, every time you move from one season to the next, the space between you changes.

||||||||||||||||||||||||

The space between you is dynamic because life is always changing, and it's also dynamic because you're married to a human being. And human beings are endlessly complex and surprising.

Out of seven billion people on the planet, you have chosen this one person to live your life with, day in and day out, year after year. You know this person. You've spent a lot of time with them. You're familiar with what they like, with what annoys them.

R: You learn that Kristen will most likely order the vegetable curry.

K: And that Rob is happiest if he's in the ocean.

R: And Kristen does not like surprise birthday parties.

K: And Rob is unable to wait to open a present. He will literally unwrap a present for him under the Christmas tree just to know what it is and then wrap it back up without telling anyone.

R: Then how did you know?

K: Intuition.

That sort of thing.

You build up these familiarities over the years. Patterns, habits, quirks, preferences, tastes—you finish each other's sentences, you know what they're thinking from across the room, you show up at breakfast both wearing a gray T-shirt with green pants and brown sandals.

You feel like they're your other half.

But then there are those moments when they surprise you.

R: You're at a dinner party and she starts telling a story you've never heard her tell and suddenly you find yourself listening from across the table thinking, "Who is this mysterious red-headed woman who tells these interesting stories?"

K: Like the time Rob told me he's going to hike across Iceland.

R: Or the time Kristen announced that she was going to Harry Potter World. I didn't see that coming.

You've spent thousands of hours with this person, and yet you can be strolling through a furniture store and suddenly they flop down in a chair and say, *I love this chair* and you say, *You do?*

There are times you get them a gift and you know it's perfect and they're going to love it, and then there are other times you have no idea how they'll react.

People aren't static; they're dynamic—endlessly complex and capable of tremendous surprise and change.

We have a friend whose father is a doctor and worked all the time and wasn't around much while she was growing up. But then, at the age of seventy, he experienced a profound spiritual rebirth that radically changed him, altering everything about his life, from how he spends his time to his connection with his family.

This surprised everyone, especially his wife, who was thrilled. At seventy years old.

There is an endless mystery to this human being you are married to, a mystery in which you never stop

learning more about this person you know better than anyone else.

This person has a body—a tangible physicality that you can see and admire and embrace. It's an exotic combination of dust and blood and skin that can be weighed and measured. They also have a soul, a spirit, a personality—a vast, intangible essence that extends way beyond whether or not they are in the room.

Sometimes when people have just met or they've gone out a few times, they'll tell their friends, *We're just getting to know each other.*

But you never stop *getting to know each other.* People who have been married for fifty years regularly turn to each other and say, *So, what'd you think?*

To be married is to be joined at the deepest levels of your being with someone who is both known and unknown, predictable and surprising.

These surprises can bring you together, and they can pull you apart; they can be endearing, and they can also be disorienting.

K: A number of years ago Rob wanted to move to a different part of town. A part of town where I didn't feel safe walking around by myself. And when Rob gets an idea in his head, he doesn't stop bringing it up—at least back then.

R: That was true.

K: But I didn't want to move there.

R: And I did, and I kept thinking: *What's the problem? Let's do this.*

K: I was baffled that he felt so strongly about this.

That's the maddening thing about marriage: you're with this person who is so similar to you, from tastes to values to worldview—otherwise, you wouldn't have married them—but then there are those moments when you wonder if they've lost their mind. How is it that you can be together on so many things and then all of the sudden they say something and you respond, *What are you talking about?*

They're like you, and then they're not like you.

You're one—you're lives and souls and bodies are intertwined and connected—but then there are those moments when it's shockingly obvious that you're two—with two opinions, two perspectives, two ways of doing things.

Whether it's something one of you wants that the other doesn't even understand, or a difficult season that came out of nowhere, or a change that one of you is going through—everything affects the space between you.

Because of the dynamic nature of the space and the complexity of the two of you, **you never stop *figuring it out.*** This is not a cliché; this is a truth about the nature of the space between you. It's always changing, and so you're always adjusting, adapting, discussing, and navigating it together.

You may have the illusion that you can *figure it out* for good, get the right things in place, master the best methods and techniques, and then you'll be all set—you will have *arrived.*

But as soon as you think you have it figured out, something will change. And you'll need to adjust and adapt and figure it out *again.*

When you get married you're starting a conversation that never ends, a conversation that includes all of the everyday details about bringing in the recycling bin and stopping by the vet to get those pills, and did you call the electrician? And at a much deeper level it's a conversation in which you never stop *figuring it out.*

You're going to try things that don't work.
You're going to say yes to things that you later regret.
You're going to spend money on something and then later realize that wasn't the best decision.

You're going to have lots of conversations in which you say to each other, *Let's not do that again.*

You're both unique, your marriage is unique, and learning what works for you will require lots and lots of talking.

And to keep talking, you have to be honest.

K: Sometimes it's not working for you. Whether it's the schedule or the pace or the responsibilities— sometimes you find yourself limping along. You can be stoic and keep it in and not say anything, but it affects the space between you.

R: And duct tape can hold things together for only so long.

K: Sometimes it feels like you can't do it all, but you "should" be able to do it all and so you just keep pretending that everything is fine.

R: Pretending is a killer.

K: That house in the other part of town that Rob wanted to move into? We moved there, and I tried to make it work, but I had to admit that it wasn't working. I remember taking a trip to Arizona during that time and sitting outside on the patio and realizing that I didn't want to go back. I knew how much Rob loved living there, but I couldn't do it anymore, and that meant I had to tell him the truth. The thought of having that conversation was gut wrenching.

R: And so she told me. And once I got through my initial shock, I had lots of questions.

K: Which is really important. Because it's easy to have an immediate, emotional reaction when someone is honest without hearing the whole story and trying to see what they see and understand where they're coming from.

R: And so we talked. And talked some more. And unexpectedly, the more I listened and the more Kristen explained, the more we ended up discussing not just the house, but the process that led us to moving in the first place.

K: And that led us into some new territory—because up until then, when we'd risked or jumped or taken a leap, we'd done it together, both of us in it all the way. Rob has a history of taking risks, and for the most part they'd turned out well. So when he started talking about this move and I had serious misgivings, I wondered whether this was just one of those times when I had to trust that he was seeing something I was missing.

R: She started talking about *where* we were living, but in a short time we found ourselves talking about *how* we were living, because it turns out that when she started telling the truth, there were a number of *other* truths behind that truth.

Moving, *wishing you hadn't moved,* conversations you didn't see coming, honesty loaded with implications, talking about issues that lead to more issues—with the two of you occupying the same space with your unique mix of personalities, let alone financial pressures and health concerns and work and family—you never stop *figuring it out.*

The question, then, that you keep returning to, the question you continually ask each other is

How's the space between us?

Sometimes there's too much distance between you, and sometimes there's not enough.

There is *one* of you and one of her or him, so together there are *two* of you who in marriage become *one.*

You're one—
but you're not the same—
as the song goes.

If there's *too much* distance between you, you can easily drift apart. It's easy to become so wrapped up in your own interests and career and even friends that you're living separate lives even though you're married. But too much distance can also happen at a more subtle level. You can be raising kids together and running a household and even owning a business or working together, and yet your interactions have a surface quality to them. Your lives are intertwined in a number of ways, and yet your hearts feel far from each other.

If there isn't *enough* distance between you, you can easily lose your sense of identity. You can find your life too absorbed in the life of another.

K: We all know women who have lost themselves in a marriage—giving up their dreams and goals and losing their sense of self in the process. Sometimes women absorb messages from their family or the culture around them or especially certain religious environments that tell her—in subtle ways, not always with words—that she's not an equal and therefore her needs and desires and aspirations are not as important as her husband's.

R: Over the years I've done lots of weddings, and in some of them the bride and groom light what's called a *unity candle.* They each take a small candle and use these two small candles to light together a third, much larger candle as a symbol of their new life together. Which is a beautiful image, to say the least, until they're done lighting the big candle—and then they often BLOW OUT their individual candles. At which point it's all I can do to *not* interrupt and say, *No! Don't do that! Don't blow out the candle that represents you; you're not going away or dying or being snuffed out.*

You're two complete and equal people, endlessly adjusting the distance between you, neither drifting apart nor losing yourselves in the other.

How's the space between us?

Sometimes it's an issue of timing. You're still living like you're in a previous season, but that season is over and now you're in a new one. You have to adjust and adapt.

You ask
What's changed?
And how is that affecting the space between us?
And how do we need to change because of that change?

IIIIIIIIIIIIIIIIIIIIIIIII

All kinds of things are going to come your way, and these changes can bring you together or drive you apart. They can be obstacles to the love and energy flowing between you, or they can become opportunities for even more flow.

With all the changes that are coming your way, let alone what's going on inside of you, it's only natural that you're going to have conflict. And fights are an excellent example of how something can bring you together or drive you apart.

Fights are all part of figuring it out. Fights are normal.

Is it normal to . . .

. . . not like this person at times?
Yes.

. . . not want to talk to them sometimes?
Yes.

. . . wonder whether they've lost their mind?
Yes.

. . . wonder whether you're losing your mind dealing with them because they've lost their mind?
Yes.

. . . wonder whether your losing your mind because of them is causing them to lose their mind even more?
Yes.

You can learn to fight well.

K: Early in our marriage I learned that when things got tense, my default reaction was to shut down and walk out of the room. Which didn't help resolve the conflict.

R: And I learned that when I could sense a fight coming on, I would immediately distract Kristen by trying to be funny. And we all know that if you're *trying* to be funny, it probably isn't that funny.

K: And it's also avoiding the issue.

R: Kind of like walking out of the room.

K: Or trying to be funny.

We all have ways we avoid conflict, and we also have *triggers* that escalate conflict. Triggers are words, phrases, and reminders that feed our fears and vulnerabilities and insecurities. These triggers activate the more primitive part of our brains, putting us in a heightened, defensive state. It's impossible to have a rational discussion in those moments, because the rational part of your brain that makes logical, wise decisions and generally says things that make sense has gotten hijacked by this more primitive part of your brain.

You can know your own triggers, and you can know theirs. Becoming aware of the triggers, talking about them, and then avoiding them can keep you out of the tornado.

R: "The tornado" is when you're arguing and something pops into your head that you could say but you know for sure that it's the worst possible thing you could say at that moment—and yet you say it.

K: Like the phrase: *You always do that.*

R: Few triggers are more explosive than that one.

You can't have a rational discussion—you can't fight well—when you are in the tornado. Just as certain words, phrases, and actions act as triggers—escalating the conflict and adding to the tension—some de-escalate tensions.

K: In the middle of a conflict when things are heated and both of us are saying things we don't mean, I tend to slip into thinking *This is who he is* rather than *This is the exception.* When I'm really angry, it helps to stop and ask myself: *Is this consistent with who I've known him to be up until now?*

When you're fighting, it's absolutely crucial to keep remembering that they're trying to figure it out just like you are. Because the space between you is dynamic, they're trying to deal with the endless changes just like you are.

K: I once heard wedding vows that had this line in them: *I will always give you the benefit of the doubt.*

You can give them the benefit of the doubt.
You can assume that they are trying to *figure it out* just like you are.

K: A friend of ours was recently telling us about how before he and his wife were divorced, they got into raging battles over him leaving the toothpaste out on the counter.

R: And another friend around that same time said that her ex-husband would blow a fuse over how she put the cap on the laundry detergent.

Of course, these weren't arguments about toothpaste and laundry detergent. When you fight, there's often an issue behind the issue. You're probably not arguing about the dining room chairs or the salad dressing or something one of you said last Tuesday. You're probably arguing about trust or responsibility or not listening or caring or making an effort.

You can learn to identify the issue behind the issue.

Past wounds, bitterness that's gone unchecked, things you haven't brought up because of shame or fear over how they'll react or insecurity because you just want them to think the best of you—you know there's an issue behind the issue when your reaction is way out of proportion to whatever it is you're fighting about.

You can keep talking and asking questions until you discover the issue behind the issue.

And you can also get really good at apologizing.

The stronger person always apologizes first. Apologizing always helps. Always. You can't go wrong apologizing. Apologizing has a mysterious way of humbling you and opening the other person up. Even saying *I'm sorry that you feel that way* is a start.

K: Sometimes what we want is just to be heard. We want to know that they've actually listened to us.

R: It's written in the scriptures that *God gives grace to the humble,* and one of the ways you see this most vividly is when you're in a heated argument and your brain is in full defense mode and the accusations are flying and you're both pulling triggers left and right . . . then one of you pauses and says, *I'm so sorry*—and something shifts.

Whatever it is you're fighting about—from money to moving to the stress of a new season—you have to start with understanding where the other person is coming from. This always involves listening, and more importantly, trying to see.

Because you have *your* eyes, *your* perspective, *your* way of seeing things. And they have *their* eyes, *their* perspective, *their* way of seeing things.

R: When we were first married and Kristen didn't see things as I did, I had this salesman gear I would shift into—persuading, selling, trying to convince.

K: I could always feel the pitch coming.

R: I'd be working so hard to get her to see or act in a particular way or agree to something—

K: —or move to a certain part of town.

R: Ouch. But true.

In those moments when the two of you see things differently, you can hold on to your view, defending it and protecting it and arguing for its superiority, or you can allow your perspective to be broadened, enriched, expanded, and deepened.

You can learn to see things from their perspective.

It's one thing in the middle of a tense discussion to say, *Why in the world do you see it that way?* which is really the question, *Why can't you see it like I do?* which is really asking, *What's wrong with you?*

It's another thing in the middle of that same tense discussion to ask, *Why do you see it that way?* by which you're also asking, *What am I missing?* which leads to *What are you seeing that I'm not seeing that I need you to help me see?*

When in doubt, assume that they're seeing something that you aren't.

When you get married, you get another set of eyes. If you aren't careful, this other set of eyes that sees the world differently can become a constant source of tension and conflict—with each of you endlessly trying to get the other to see everything like you do and win them over to your view.

You can let your different ways of seeing give you a broader, wider, fuller view of the world. Instead of seeing with two eyes, you're now seeing with four.

R: I remember sitting on that patio in Arizona listening to Kristen tell me that she didn't want to continue living in that house I had so badly wanted us to live in. A part of me wanted to argue my case and change her mind, but as I kept asking questions, I gradually found myself seeing things I hadn't seen up until that moment.

K: As we continued the discussion over the following weeks, we realized that the house was the issue that got us talking, but there were issues behind that issue.

You can change the way you see challenges, surprises, and conflicts. You can learn to see them as opportunities for the bonds between you to grow stronger.

This is especially true when it comes to issues that often create the most conflict in marriage. For example, money.

During some seasons, you have more money, and during some you have less. Sometimes you have no idea how you're going to make ends meet, and other times you have extra—and you each have strong opinions about how it should be spent. With all of the issues money inevitably brings your way, there is always potential for great conflict *or* bonding.

K: When we got married, some people gave us money as wedding gifts. I had a whole list of things in mind I thought we should spend it on. My new husband, on the other hand, got really excited about buying a new guitar.

You discover in marriage that when you're talking about money, you're talking about lots of other things. And the more quickly you can identify those other things, the better.

K: We learned right away that our conflicts about money—

R: and guitars

K: —stemmed from our different personalities, the perspectives on money we'd grown up with, and our priorities for our life together. Rob is the eternal optimist. He assumes there's plenty, and if there isn't, he assumes there will be.

R: Kristen is disciplined and organized and conscientious and a number of other things I admire. It's very important to her to have a plan that makes sense that will avoid unnecessary problems.

We were newly married and both of us were in graduate school, and we didn't have much money. We sat down and wrote out all of our expenses. We then listed the money we did have and the money we would be getting from our jobs. It was eye-opening for both of us. And then together we figured out how we were going to make it all work. Boundaries and budgets and clarity and transparency free you from tension, revealing how much money there actually is and how much you can spend.

Throughout the course of your marriage, you will have unexpected expenses.

K: From speeding tickets—

R: That was just once . . .

K: —to your refrigerator breaking.

Moments when you get the bill and you look at each other and say, *Seriously?*

You will also find things on sale and people will give you unexpected gifts and there may be a tax refund you didn't know was coming and you may even get a raise or a bonus at some point. You may make money when you sell a house, and you may lose money when you sell a house. You will make mistakes that cost you money, and you will make wise decisions with your money.

You can continually remind each other that it's just money, and you can remind each other that nobody gets it right every time because you never stop figuring it out.

You never stop figuring it out because every marriage is unique. You listen and talk and discuss and try things as you work out what it looks like for the two of you to build a life together.

K: It's easy to get frustrated because you feel like your marriage—or your life—isn't working, but you're not able to articulate why. When things weren't working for me, I'd often tell Rob that I felt overwhelmed.

R: Which didn't give me much to go on.

When you bring them a vague cloud of ambiguous feelings and impulses, it's hard for them to help. Do you feel neglected? Do you think you're carrying too much of the weight? Do they seem distant? Is it time to take the next step in your career and you need their help? Are you stressed because you've taken on too much?

It's really important that you do your absolute best to articulate what isn't working for you—without attaching unnecessary emotion to it.

Put some thought into it. If you're frustrated, it can easily come out *reactive* instead of *proactive*. Reactive says, *You don't care and you're not helping me.* Proactive says, *How can we make this better?*

R: It took me a while to realize that whenever Kristen articulated what wasn't working for her, I immediately got defensive. As if anything *she* said about things not working for *her* was a statement about me not being, you know, The Man. Like I had failed her in some way. But I learned over time that she didn't see it that way.

It's not about failure; it's about trying to figure it out with this person who is committed to figuring it out with you.

Honesty can be terrifying. If you actually sit down and listen, you may hear things that are hard to hear. It takes courage to be honest, and it also takes courage to listen.

Great marriages have an ease about them, a back-and-forth nonreactive, nondefensive, open, and ongoing flow in which you never stop talking and figuring it out together.

As you do this, you'll discover that events and circumstances you never saw coming or never would have wished for have the unexpected ability to bring you together in ways you never would have imagined. There is a divine mystery to how this works.

R: The Bible begins with a poem about water. Water in the ancient world was a picture of the dark, the unexpected, the unknown. But in this poem, God creates something new and good from out of the water.

K: Something beautiful comes from the dark and unknown and unexpected.

You can see every change—every new season—as an opportunity to grow closer together. You can allow differences between you to expand your perspective.

The space between you is dynamic because life is dynamic. The changes will never stop coming, and they will always bring with them the potential for the love to flow between you all the more freely. You can get tense and dig in your heels and react negatively, or you can be limber and flexible, reminding each other that you're in it together, there's no need to panic, something new will come out of it, something *good*.

CHAPTER 4

EXCLUSIVE

The space between you is responsive, it's dynamic, and it's also **exclusive.** We use the word *exclusive* because the space that exists between the two of you exists nowhere else in the universe.

There are about seven billion other people on the planet, and when you zimzum for just this one person and that person zimzums for you, it creates space that you have with no one else. This space can be a tremendous source of life and safety and grounding and love.

We've drawn exclusive with the circle going around the two stick figures because this space can be strengthened and protected. When you strengthen and protect it, you increase the flow of love and energy between you.

In the winter of 2008 we were flying home from Costa Rica with our boys, and we had a layover in Houston. It was dinnertime and we were hungry and the food court was hot and crowded.

R: There were long lines, so Kristen and the boys found a seat while I ordered our food. While I was waiting, I noticed a man in line hand the cashier a piece of paper. The cashier read it and then began entering in his order, until she stopped and pointed at something the man had written. He read it and then turned around and made eye contact with his wife sitting at one of the tables and began signing something to her. He then turned and pointed to something on the paper, the cashier asked him something else, he turned around and continued conversing in sign language with his wife. It was beautiful to watch. People standing between them actually backed up a bit to give them more space to see each other, many of them watching as riveted as we were.

K: In the midst of that cramped, loud food court full of people trying to get home, it was like everything slowed down and it was just the two of them *as if they were the only two people in the airport.* You could almost see the exclusive circle around them.

In quantum physics, when two subatomic particles have been bonded and then separated, they demonstrate an awareness of each other *after* they've been disconnected. This is called *entanglement.* There's a quantum entanglement dimension to marriage—you're connected and intertwined at a mysterious level. It's that thing that happens when you know what they're going to say before they say it, or when you're apart and you feel them with you in spirit.

When you strengthen this exclusive bond, the flow and energy between you is increased. **One of the primary ways you strengthen this bond is through shared experiences.**

In 2006 we were in South Africa and our friend Theo said, "Would you like to go shark diving?" Of course we said yes, and so we got on a boat that took us out onto the ocean. The crew dropped anchor and then lowered a cage over the boat's side. The captain asked who wanted to get in the cage first.

R: I turned around and laughed because Kristen was already putting on a wetsuit.

K: I knew that it was one of those moments that if I didn't do it, I'd regret it later. And when else was I planning on being in South Africa about to climb over the side of a boat into a cage that was surrounded by great white sharks?

The captain then took out a huge piece of chum and hooked it on the end of a stick and dragged it through the water to attract sharks.

K: My heart was beating so hard.

The sharks would swim right at the cage and then swerve at the last second. Which meant that there were these moments when you were eye to eye with a great white.

K: The current was really strong, and I had to hang on so my hands wouldn't slip through the bars on the cage that were at least a foot apart.

R: My hands and feet did slip through several times.

There was this kid from Mexico on the boat who was climbing over the edge to get in the cage at the exact moment the captain dragged the chum too close and a shark slammed into the side of the boat.

K: I've never heard Spanish spoken like that.

After several hours of taking turns in the cage, we noticed the wind picking up and the captain getting increasingly agitated. He then pulled the cage up into the boat and announced that we were going in because a storm was coming. As we headed to shore, the waves got bigger and bigger until the entire front of the boat was submerged each time we hit a new wave. When that happened, you could see clearly underwater *through the windshield.*

When we finally made it to shore, someone who knew our driver asked whether we could take a box back to town for him. Our driver said yes, so he put the box in the back of the car with us, and off we went. Several miles down the road, we heard a noise coming from that box. We listened more intently and heard the noise again.

So we did what anyone would do in that situation: we opened the box and saw that it was full of . . . penguins.

K: I remember sitting there in the backseat, looking over at Rob and realizing that we didn't need to say a word because we both knew what the other was thinking.

R: We were giving each other that *box-full-of-penguins* look.

Some looks are more than just a look because some moments are about more than just that particular moment. That look contained more than just the *box-full-of-penguins* look; it also contained the depth of all the experiences we've shared over the years, the thousands of those kinds of looks we've given each other. We were laughing about the box full of penguins, but there was a laugh behind the laugh—one that came from the accumulated effect of all those moments when we've experienced something new or strange or exhilarating together. **When you are first with someone, you only have a few experiences—but over time, they build up, forming a collective memory that exists exclusively between the two of you.**

This is one of the ways that you become one. Your personal histories are increasingly linked together, filling the space between you with common stories and impressions and events. They're like glue, bonding you together.

In 2009 we were in the White House with our six-month-old daughter, just outside the Oval Office, when the friend who was showing us around had to step away for a minute. We noticed that the door to the Rose Garden wasn't locked and no one was around, so we went outside. We were standing there giving each other the *how-did-we-end-up-alone-in-the-Rose-Garden?* look, which, by the way, is very similar to the *box-full-of-penguins* look—when we realized that our daughter desperately needed a diaper change. And this wasn't something that could wait. To this day, whenever we see a picture of that portico that presidents walk under to give a speech, we smile and look at each other and think: *Been there. Changed a diaper there.*

There are these moments in marriage—sometimes in the middle of exotic and thrilling experiences, other times in the course of an average day—when you're reminded all over again of the extraordinary gift you've been given in this person.

In the mornings we make our kids' breakfast together, on Sunday evenings we get groceries, on Fridays we work out together, and on weeknights after we put our daughter to bed we take our dog for a walk. And when we walk, we talk—about everything—from our kids to what's coming in the days ahead to something that's driving one of us crazy and we just need to vent, to something interesting we heard or read that we want to discuss.

That's the power of the exclusive space—there is this person you get to share your life with. You are not alone. Someone is witnessing your life while you're witnessing theirs. Someone is noticing and paying attention in a way no one else is.

What are the things that just the two of you share? You can strengthen the exclusive space between you through shared experiences.

Sometimes people say that they want to *work* on their marriage. And that's important. But it also may be the wrong verb. You can *work on* your marriage, but you can also *play at* your marriage.

When you consistently think and act in certain ways, particular neural pathways are formed in your brain. Every time you repeat those thoughts or actions, you are reinforcing those pathways as the myelin sheaths around the nerves grow thicker and stronger. Over time, it becomes harder and harder for you to think and act in other ways. This is called a rut.

Sometimes the space between you isn't humming, and what you need is a jolt, a shock, a trip, a class, a book— whatever it takes to form that new neural pathway, the one that will help you see this person you're committed to in a new light.

In 2001 a friend of ours opened a yoga studio near our house, and we started going to her classes. Neither of us had practiced yoga before, and we quickly learned all sorts of new language and awareness of how integrated our minds and bodies and spirits are and how central breathing is to *everything.*

It was stunning how just one hour a week infused our entire life together with new energy. From sharks to penguins to yoga to sharing a magazine article at breakfast—when you intentionally set out to learn and grow and experience new things together, it brings new energy to the flow between you.

When we got married, we had this sense that we were going on an adventure together, that our life with each other would above all else be *interesting.*

A marriage can easily devolve into a kind of business partnership—raising kids, running a household, keeping things going. It can quickly be swallowed up with taxes and carpools and trips to Home Depot and maybe Bed Bath & Beyond if you have enough time. You each know your roles—you pay bills, take kids to soccer practice, pull weeds, sort the mail—but over time it gets old, a low-grade monotony sets in, and the spark that brought you together in the beginning is lost.

This loss is a fear that lurks on the edges of quite a few bachelor and bachelorette parties. Often, they're planned months in advance, sometimes involving a trip to Las Vegas or Miami or Uncle Rick's cabin. The wedding party goes away and gets *wild and crazy* because somebody is getting married—the implicit understanding being that their carefree and spontaneous days are over and this is their last chance to live it up.

Bachelor parties are a reflection of how people see marriage.

Often, the understanding is that being married is the end of a phase of life in which you were free—free to explore and have new experiences—and the start of a new phase in which you're limited, hindered, chained (the phrase *ball and chain* comes from somewhere)—because now you have responsibilities, you've settled down.

But marriage is about adventure. It's not about what you're *losing,* it's what you're *gaining.* You're gaining someone to go on adventures with, someone to explore the world with, someone who's up for stepping out into the unknown with you. We've looked at each other countless times and said, *Let's try it and see what happens.* How you *see* marriage has extraordinary power to shape how you *experience* marriage.

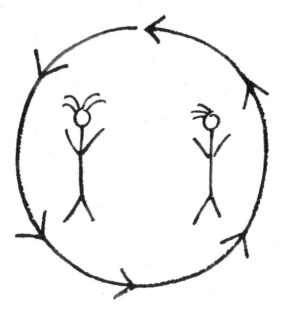

Shared experiences are held by the two of you within the circle—they strengthen your bond; they connect you to each other; they create the knowing glances, the inside jokes, the phrases that only you know what they mean.

R: Like when Kristen says she needs to *drive fast with the windows down*—I know exactly what's going on with her.

K: Or when Rob tells me that *the black dog has come for a visit.*

Shared experiences are the fuel for the energetic movement between you.

You also strengthen the exclusive space between you when you let them in to your life in ways you let no one else in.

You each have an interior life—doubts, fears, insecurities, issues you're sorting out, wounds that are healing, hopes and dreams you have. No matter how confident or strong or successful we may be appear, we're all a jumble of vulnerabilities and questions trying to make sense of what it means to be *us*.

K: A friend of ours who has interviewed a number of world leaders and famous personalities says that they often ask her afterward, *How did I do? Was I okay?*

We've drawn exclusive with the couple being encircled because over time the bonds between you create a place of trust, safety, and belonging—a place where you feel free to be yourself as you find your path.

When we walk our dog after putting our daughter to bed, it's just a walk, and yet it's more than just a walk. It's another opportunity for us to let each other in. You let them into your thoughts and your fears and what makes you happy and what makes you angry. You ask for advice. You vent about something that's bothering you. When you do this repeatedly over time, it creates increasingly safe space between you, space that exists nowhere else in the universe but between the two of you.

There's a great line from a song by Edward Sharpe and the Magnetic Zeroes:

Home, home is whenever I'm with you.

When you strengthen this exclusive space between you, it becomes like a home. It's familiar, it's safe, it's where you belong. You return to it again and again.

||||||||||||||||||||||

You can strengthen this exclusive space, and you can also *protect* it.

Years ago we went on a trip with a couple who joked about each other constantly. At first, the sarcasm was funny, and so we laughed along with them because it's all in good fun, right? But as it continued, the slights became less funny and more disturbing. They never seemed to stop with the digs and jabs and barbed comments about the shortcomings and faults of the other. As the week went on, we realized that their sarcasm was rooted in unresolved issues between them. And when they joked about each other to us, they were essentially bringing us into their space—space where we didn't belong.

To protect the space between you, don't let people in where they don't belong.

When you have a fight or an unresolved issue, it's only between the two of you. The two of you need to work it out. If you vent to your best friend or Mom or co-worker about your husband or wife, you have let that person into your exclusive space. They don't belong there, because whatever the two of you have, it's between the two of you.

If it's a fight about a larger struggle or pattern, one that keeps coming up and you can't seem to get a handle on it, you may need to see a counselor or therapist or mentor or spiritual leader, intentionally bringing a professional or expert into this particular issue at this time for this specific reason.

Beyond bringing an expert in, when you have a fight, it's *your* fight.

Some things shouldn't be shared with others because such sharing diminishes the power of the exclusive circle.

You're quantumly entangled, and how you talk about your partner directly affects the bonds between you. This is true when it's just the two of you; this is true when the two of you are with others; and it's also true when your partner isn't around. Complaining about your partner to your kids or to your friends or your extended family members or your neighbors is toxic. It brings people in where they don't belong.

Picture a couple at a dinner party and the wife is telling a story and the husband makes eye contact with you and rolls his eyes because he thinks she's taking too long to make her point. This may seem harmless and all in good fun, but in that moment he's doing something destructive. He has an issue with her talking too much, and instead of keeping it between them, he's bringing you in. And in doing so, he's violating their exclusive space.

Some experiences belong to just the two of you, and it's important to keep them between the two of you.

This is why reality television shows can be so awkward and fascinating at the same time: the camera goes into places where we intuitively know we don't belong. When the exclusive space between two people is entered by others—and exposed and inspected and dissected and filmed—those two people are left with less and less that is theirs alone. Reality shows can be extremely entertaining, but at an excruciatingly high cost.

Whatever belongs to just the two of you that you decide to share with others no longer belongs to just the two of you.

This is especially true of sex. Sex is exclusive—you don't reveal yourself like this to anyone else. It's more than just bodies coming together; it's entire beings coming together, the culmination of all the layers of your lives lived together. It's the highest expression of connection with another human being.

When you talk about sex with other people, sharing details and telling stories, you're diminishing and trivializing the power of what exists only between the two of you.

What you share with other people and how you look at other people and how you think about other people all affect the exclusive space between you and the one person you have given yourself fully to. You have to be ruthless about guarding your eyes and your heart and your mind and your imagination because what you have with that one person you have with no one else.

R: It's interesting that a show like *Downton Abbey* has gained such a massive following. It's about another era when people were much more reserved and had stronger cultural codes defining what was proper to share and what should remain between two people.

K: The contrast with our culture of oversharing is striking. Today, couples write love notes to each other on Facebook. In what other era were love notes publicly broadcast? Isn't the point of a love note that only one person will read it because you wrote it to only that one person?

Some experiences belong to just the two of you, and when you keep it that way, you infuse the space between you with energy.

You protect the space because if you aren't careful, you can end up with all sorts of things—and people—in the exclusive space between you.

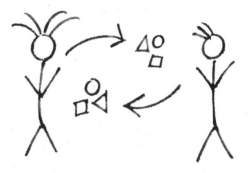

And few things will block the flow of love and energy more than another person in the space between you. This problem is as old as marriage itself, and in the Hebrew tradition there's a fascinating way of understanding how this can happen. It's written in the book of Genesis that when you get married *you leave—and then you cleave.*

R: *Cleave* is an awesome word. You rarely hear it. I love that word.

Most modern biblical translations have something like this:

A man will leave his father and mother
and be united to his wife.

In the Orthodox Jewish Bible it's written as:

Therefore shall an ish leave his av and his em
and shall cleave unto his isha
and they shall be basar echad.

Man is *ish* in Hebrew,
woman is *isha*,
your mom and dad are your *av* and *em*,
and you leave them and cling.

R: Cleave!

And you become *basar echad,* which literally means *one*
flesh. You leave, and then you cleave, and the two of you
become one flesh.

We all have families of origin. Some are biological; some
we've adopted along the way. Moms and dads and
brothers and sisters and cousins and roommates and
neighbors and co-workers—these are the people we are
closest to in the world. They're the ones we lean on, learn
from, and spend most of our time with.

These primary bonds shape us in untold ways, from how
we think about money to loyalty to religion to how we

vote. But then you fall in love, and you zimzum for this person who has their own family of origin and their own primary bonds that have shaped them significantly as well.

For your marriage to thrive, a fundamental shift must occur in your primary bonds. You've always been a son or a daughter or a brother, sister, or friend—and you always will be—but now you will need to learn what it looks like to be a son or a daughter or a brother, sister, or friend in this new reality you find yourself in, because you are now a husband or a wife *first*.

This new relationship now has priority. If you don't leave and cleave well, it's easy to end up with other people in the space between you.

Sometimes it's past partners. They're still there, haunting the space, their shadow looming large over the two of you.

Sometimes it's family members who continue unhealthy attachments or controlling behaviors.

Sometimes it's friends who don't have boundaries or an awareness that your life is different from the way it used to be.

Sometimes it's kids. When you cleave well, you create an airtight bond that is your primary relationship. Bringing kids into the world can easily disrupt this primary bond, making it feel like the kids have come between you.

Whoever is in the space between you and however they got there, it's absolutely crucial that you are honest about how their presence is affecting the space between you. It's your exclusive space, and if you feel like someone's in the space, you need to talk about it.

How do you know when there's no one else in the space between you? When you both agree that there's no one else in the space between you.

It isn't just *people* who can be in your space; things that you brought with you from your past can be there, too.

Our therapist once gave us each a sheet of paper on which was written a list of words like *Christmas* and *money* and *vacation* and *forgiveness* and *sex.* He then told us to write down whatever associations or expectations came to mind when we read those words.

It was extremely illuminating for us to see how different some of our expectations were and how much our pasts had shaped us differently.

When you get married, you each bring with you a number of assumptions and expectations about what your life together will look like—some that you may not even be aware of. Sometimes you have conflict because you're operating in the way you used to and you haven't properly left that way in order to be open to the new way you are creating together.

You can examine your assumptions, peeling back the layers to discover the expectations and motivations behind your actions. You're creating a new life together, one that may look a lot like the families you come from, or that may not. Whatever it looks like, it's for you to create together.

IIIIIIIIIIIIIIIIIIIIIIIIII

Our friend Sister Virginia is a member of the School Sisters of Notre Dame, and one of the vows she took to become a sister is the vow of celibacy. She explains her vow by saying that she loves God by loving everybody equally—she calls it *loving the One through the many*. She often used to tell us that *our* lives were different because when we married each other, we made a decision *to love the many through the one*.

Love the One through the many?
Love the many through the one?

You have energies. And you have options for how you're going to spend those energies. Work and play and friends and family and hobbies and causes—there's no end to the ways we can give our energies to the world.

When you zimzum, you are consciously deciding to give your energies first and foremost to one person. That's the power of the exclusive space—out of seven billion people on the planet, you first give yourself to just this *one* person in just this one way. You direct your love and will and energy to this *one*.

Like a laser beam, when you direct and focus your energies, they intensify. And when the two of you direct and focus your energies on each other, you create an extraordinary energy field between you. It's the buzz, the crackle, the electricity that hums between you. When we describe the exclusive space, it's important to understand that this is not about the two of you endlessly gazing into each other's eyes. It's not ultimately about the two of you.

As you intentionally take action for the well-being of this person you love, strengthening and protecting the exclusive space between you, something unexpected happens.

Your love overflows.

Your love and sacrifice and devotion take you not just beyond yourself, but beyond the two of you. The energy that is generated between you transcends the two of you. By first committing to just each other, you naturally create something that is bigger than you both.

This is why marriage is good for the world. Love that overflows makes the world a better place. It's a gift—a beautiful, divine, sacred gift to the world.

CHAPTER 5

SACRED

The space between you is responsive, dynamic, and exclusive. It's also **sacred.**

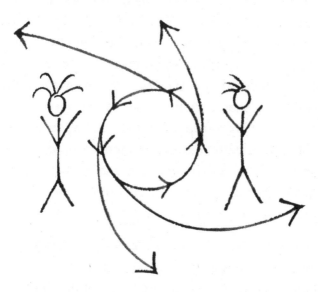

We've drawn sacred with the arrows starting *between* you and then moving *beyond* you because that's how the mystery of marriage works. It's just the two of you, and yet what's happening between you points you way beyond just the two of you. The love that flows between you in this sacred space is reflective of the divine love that flows through all of creation.

The more aware you are of how sacred this space is, the more this love can flow freely between you.

R: Something happened to me that first weekend in Los Angeles when Kristen came to visit. Even now, as I try to describe it more than twenty years later, I find it difficult to put into words. It was a Saturday afternoon and we were at my grandma's apartment discussing what we wanted to do that evening. We talked about lots of options and eventually decided to drive out to Malibu and then eat dinner in Santa Monica. I remember standing in the hallway—which had yellow shag carpeting that hadn't been updated in years so when you vacuumed it you had to be careful that chunks didn't disappear—and realizing that our discussion had been effortless. I know that may sound like a rather basic observation, but for me, at that time, it was revolutionary.

K: There was no drama, no pretending, no hidden agendas—it felt like everything was in its right place. It didn't matter to me where we went or what we did; there was a natural flow to being together that I didn't want to end.

R: I stood there in that hallway overwhelmed with the stillness that had come over my entire being. With Kristen, I could breathe. I could relax. I could be myself. I didn't have to prove anything. I didn't have to be anybody or anything else. I felt a peace in her presence unlike any I had ever experienced. It was like coming home.

K: We had known each other for a long time, but that weekend everything changed. I knew that I loved him.

R: There was something about being with her that made me think differently about all of life. It was her, but it was more than just her.

K: It was just the two of us, and yet what was going on between us pointed us way beyond just the two of us.

R: There's a word for what I was experiencing standing there in that hallway—the word is *grace.*

Grace is when you aren't striving or controlling or trying to change or manipulate or make something happen. Grace is when you find yourself carried along, when all that's left to do is receive. Grace is when you know you're loved, exactly as you are. Grace is an entirely different way of experiencing life.

Another word for *grace* is *gift.*

We were at our neighborhood Thai restaurant the other night when a guy we know came in with his date—he often has a new date—and they sat two tables over from us. He has a loud voice, and with great flourish he picked out the wine and walked her through his favorite items on the menu, and then he began telling her about his varied interests, including the poetry that he writes, poetry that, he wanted her to know, *just pours out of my heart.*

It was, as you can imagine, quite a performance.

And that's the problem. Dating can easily be about showing and impressing and giving this person sitting across the table from you a particular, well-crafted impression of who you want them to think you are. But it's more than just dating. Much of life can be about presenting a controlled and edited image of ourselves, an image in which we are smart and successful and have it all together.

But what we long for, what we really want, is someone who will see our best *and our worst*—and still want to be with us.

K: In one survey of unmarried men, some of them said they were looking for a fling, but the majority said they were looking for someone who would rub their back while they threw up.

We're all aware of the thoughts that race through our minds about our faults and failures and shame and insecurities and anger and secrets and all the

deepest darkest whatevers that we're carrying around—
all those things we're most terrified people might find out
about us.

R: Like when you're arguing and there's this thing on the
tip of your tongue that you're tempted to say but you
know it's absolutely the worst possible thing you could
say at that moment but once it enters your brain you
can't stop thinking about it and you feel helpless to
stop it and then you actually do say it and as soon as
it hits her ears your worst suspicions are confirmed
that it actually was the worst possible thing you ever
could have said and so you beat yourself up about it
and you can't figure out where that came from and
you're so frustrated with yourself—and this person
you love, who matters more to you than anyone else,
heard it all.

K: In marriage there is no edited version.

Grace doesn't brush over our sins and failures and
faults—it sees them clearly in all their Technicolor mess.
There's a great line in the Psalms about grace and truth
meeting together. This is what we want—someone to fully
see the truth about us—shadows and all—and still love us
and accept us and embrace us.

Something beautiful happens in marriage when this
person you're with knows the truth about you and still
loves you exactly as you are, extending grace to you

time and time again. The space between you is sacred because when they do this, they're showing you what God is like.

IIIIIIIIIIIIIIIIIIIIIIII

This helps explain the mysterious, spiritual nature of sex. In sex, you are embracing and accepting another human being in actual flesh and blood. When you come together with nothing hidden, each of you saying to the other, *You are known to me and you are loved*—it is grace experienced in your entire being.

Sex is spiritual because you are an integrated being. Your skin and your soul are connected. This is why casual hookups leave people so profoundly empty—there's nothing behind them. This other person hasn't truly known you enough to give the embrace the weight and significance that it deserves. And so people walk home early the next morning with a certain heaviness in their steps, deep in the letdown of a promise that couldn't deliver.

Sex involves all of you—your mind, your spirit, your heart, your soul, your body—because you don't just *have* a body, you *are* a body. **And how you think about your body is directly related to how you experience grace.**

In the poem that begins the Bible, God is thrilled with the physicality of things—earthy, sweaty, sexy, skin-and-bones creation is good and is to be enjoyed and celebrated. This is the heart of the Christian story about Jesus—that the divine takes on flesh and blood (a body) and comes among us, the ultimate affirmation of the material world.

Spirituality is not about escape from the body or this world; it's about being fully present in it.

K: Women are bombarded literally thousands of times a day with messages about how they are not X or Y or Z enough. That their body, in other words, is not good. These messages never let up—from magazines to television to the voices in our heads telling us we fall short of perfection. For many, the only time they think about their body is when they are criticizing it. Something powerful happens when you celebrate who you are and what you have—namely, your body. It is a fascinating mix of dust and spirit, and it is yours and it is good.

Central to your experience of the sacred space between you is your care of and connection with and gratitude for your body. Fixating on what you don't like about your body is toxic for you, and for the one you love. You are quantumly entangled in marriage, and your thoughts about yourself greatly affect the space between you.

Any thought—however trivial or fleeting it is—about who or what you *aren't* takes directly away from who and what you *are*.

K: Sexy is when you feel comfortable in your own skin.

And because you don't just have a body, you are a body, everything relating to your body affects everything else in your life. Eating good food and getting plenty of exercise and sleep fill you with life and energy. You have more to give to each other because you feel better about yourself and your life together. Your body is good, everything related to your body affects everything else in your life, and through sex you're experiencing grace in the most tangible of ways.

Sex is spiritual—a living, breathing, flesh-and-blood experience of grace.

‖‖‖‖‖‖‖‖‖‖‖‖‖‖‖‖‖‖‖‖

Grace is sacred, and so is forgiveness.

It is inevitable that you will hurt each other. Whether it's something they said or something she did or something you wish he would have done but didn't do, it all creates hurts that we carry around with us.

And carrying around wounds always affects the space, blocking the flow between you.

The Greek word for *forgive* is actually two words attached to each other: the word *send* and the word *away*. To forgive is to send away.

For the love to flow between you, you need to keep forgiving each other, sending away whatever has come between you.

To forgive, you first have to name the hurt. It may be an actual phrase they used or an action they took; other times, it may be a feeling that you pick up. Whatever it is, you can't send it away if you don't know what it is. Sometimes people are wounded but they can't identify what the wound actually is, and so they carry around a vague cloud of pain while their heart grows cold.

Forgiving is a decision, and it's also a process. You decide that you're going to send away whatever it is so that it is no longer between you. This may happen instantly, without them even knowing they hurt you; other times, it may take a while. Some wounds heal in the moment; others require a bit of time.

You both can get better at sending things away. Forgiving is like a muscle that gets stronger the more you use it. There is something divine at work in those moments when you forgive, as it's written in the scriptures, *God is love* and *love covers over a multitude of sins*. When you forgive, you're showing each other what God is like.

IIIIIIIIIIIIIIIIIIIIIIIII

This person you are married to is extraordinary.

They're a human being—a finite, flawed, fragile, featherless biped, made of dust and bone and blood and water. They sometimes do things that get on your nerves; they have odd quirks and occasionally say things that make no sense; but there are these moments—maybe at the end of a long and difficult day when you're exhausted and weary, or maybe after you've tried something and you've failed and you feel about an inch tall—there are these moments when you tell that person what you're thinking and what you're feeling and you open up your heart to them and then they wrap their arms around you and tell you you're okay and things are going to be fine.

And here's the stunning part: *you believe them*. We can easily lose our centers, wandering off in our pain and confusion, conjuring up hundreds of scenarios in our minds about why it's all going to fall apart. But then this person is there for you, present in your life, reminding you of what matters. They're just a human being, and yet their consistent love and presence have the ability to both ground you and take you beyond yourself.

This is why so many love songs refer to the sun and moon and stars. The love of another human being has the profound capacity to connect us with realities as wide as the universe. *Something about their love teaches us about all love.* Through them, our view of *everything* is shaped. Returning to this same person again and again has a way of forming our deepest beliefs about the kind of world we're living in.

We have no idea what life will bring. We long for someone to be there for us, through thick and thin, to not leave us or forsake us. When life goes according to our plans and when those plans blow up in our face, we long for that someone who is there for us again and again, someone who is faithful to us. And when they are, they show us what God is like.

We've drawn sacred with the arrows radiating out because marriage is more than just two people sharing the same home, hoping they can get along, trying to stay together. In marriage you're experiencing spiritual realities through each other.

When we talk about something being spiritual or the space between you being sacred, we're talking about the sense you have that there is depth to your experiences. From a kiss to a sunset to a meal to a body to a marriage—the physical realities that we encounter have a way of pointing beyond themselves to deeper, divine realities like grace and forgiveness and trust and hope.

When you see the space as sacred, it affects the flow of love between you. You realize that there's depth to what's going on between the two of you.

In the Hebrew scriptures, there's a particular word that's used to describe the *oneness* between two people in marriage. It's the word *echad,* and it refers to oneness that contains multiple parts. *Two* people who are *one.*

This same word *echad* is also used in the scriptures to describe God. God is a community of oneness. Many people have a *static* view of God, often rooted in an image of an old man who is sitting somewhere far away, intervening in the world from time to time. But mostly sitting. Alone. Others don't believe in God, and when they articulate why, they describe their inability to believe in a God who sounds a lot like this *static* God. In these static understandings of God, there isn't any movement or momentum; God just *is.* Or isn't.

That's not the picture of God that emerges in the Bible. God is described as a *relationship* of *one.* Early theologians called this relational oneness of God *trinity.* God is movement, motion, energy, generosity—a *trinitarian* community of infinite love, endlessly moving beyond for the good of others. In this trinitarian understanding of God, love is the engine of the universe, the life force that surges through all of creation. The nature of love is that it can't be contained; it spills over and naturally creates new space for others to thrive.

This love takes us back to that first impulse you had to zimzum for this person you love. When you zimzum, you are aligning yourself with the most foundational creative energies of the universe. You're experiencing the same love that sustains the world.

The space between you is sacred because when you live beyond yourself, orienting yourself around the thriving of another, you are reflecting the image of God. You are unleashing in the space between you the same divine energies that continue to create the universe.

R: I've done weddings in fields and in prisons and on snowboards and on beaches and in backyards and even some in church buildings—and the same thing happens in every single one of them. As the bride approaches the groom—and I've seen brides come in on horses, kick open the doors to the *Stars Wars* theme, be escorted by someone in full ninja gear— every time, no matter how funny or serious or formal or weird the setting is, there is a certain—and I use this word intentionally—*tenderness* that comes over the congregation. People smile. And not just some people. Everybody smiles—even grumpy relatives. It's a smile mixed with a particular kind of expectancy and openness that you rarely see in public places.

We are moved at weddings, sometimes inexplicably, because two people giving themselves to each other speaks to us about how the universe works. We're well aware that many marriages don't last. We know there's a possibility that this couple we're watching get married might end up getting divorced. We know they're both taking a huge risk in committing to each other.

And yet we still cheer them on. We do this because we intuitively know that this risk they're taking is where the life is. Whenever you create something, there is the chance that it will fall apart, the possibility that your heart will be broken.

Their risk is a reflection of a larger divine risk. God zimzums, creating space for the world to exist and thrive. When you create space for another to thrive, it always unleashes new energies, and it always comes with risk. That's where the power of a wedding ceremony comes from: We are witnesses to the creation of something new in the world, and creation always involves risk.

No matter how much heartbreak someone has experienced, no matter how weary or cynical a person is, no matter how many times someone has been married, we stand there as these two people exchange vows, and we smile because we know that their risk has great potential for good for the world.

We're spiritual beings, reflecting the image of the God who is one, and when you commit to another and then continually extend grace to each other, year after year, conflict after conflict, the love between you becomes a grounded center from which love flows outward. As you allow this divine love to flow *between* you, it inevitably flows *through* you both, spilling over into the world around you.

There's a lot that's broken in the world, a lot that isn't *one.* From war and racism and injustice to abuse and addiction and people taking each other to court and families breaking apart. We live in a broken, fractured, fragmented world.

But when you are faithful to each other, zimzuming as you act for the well-being of the other, the space between you becomes a place in the universe that isn't broken and divided but *one* and *whole.* This is why the world needs marriage—more marriages, better marriages. The world needs more places that are one and whole. Great marriages shine, they stand out, they inspire, they bring hope, they speak to our deepest desires for a world that is one.

The arrows begin in the space between you and then move out beyond you because there is a larger purpose to your marriage. There's a point, a mission, a reason for your marriage—one that shapes each of you into better people as it makes the world a better place.

EPILOGUE

In the summer of 2008 we found out that Kristen was
pregnant. We were both thirty-eight at the time, and
we were ecstatic that nine years after the birth of our
younger son, we'd be having another baby.

R: One night in February, five months into the pregnancy,
Kristen woke up in the middle of the night struggling
for breath. She'd been finding it harder and harder
to breathe over the previous few weeks, but this
was something different. She sat perfectly still on
the edge of the bed, taking long and slow breaths,
repeatedly saying, *I don't think I'm going to make it.*
I sat there helplessly, trying to will her lungs to open
enough to get the air they needed. It was horrible.
Each of those breaths felt like it took a lifetime. We
rushed to the hospital where she spent the night
undergoing a number of tests, only to learn that the
doctors couldn't identify what was wrong, other than
pregnancy-induced asthma. They gave her an oxygen
tank and sent us home.

K: I was terrified.

R: After that, Kristen often woke up in the night, unable to breathe, repeating, *I'm not going to make it, I'm not going to make it.*

K: You know that feeling when you're a kid and you're swimming and you get held under the water for a split second longer than you were planning and your whole body floods with panic and you think you're going to drown? I had that feeling ten to twenty times a day.

R: All I could do was just sit there, hoping she'd get the air she needed. We went to a number of doctors, one of whom said that in all her years of practicing, she'd never seen *this.*

K: Because they didn't know what was causing it, my worst fear was that I would be like this for the rest of my life. And I had this ugly breathing tube attached to my nose.

R: Which helped because if I wanted to find her in the house, I just followed the hose.

K: It was the first time in our marriage when I had nothing to give. Rob had to take over caring for the kids, doing laundry, shopping for groceries, bringing me everything I needed. I didn't like being alone, and so Rob stayed with me. Every Friday night, every Saturday night, every night for that matter, Rob stayed in and kept me company. But it wasn't just that, it was the vertigo that came from our relationship being so one-sided. Up until that time, there had always been a sense that we were creating a life together. But all of a sudden I found myself giving all of my energies to simply surviving. It was very, very difficult to accept this.

R: Grace.

K: Yes, grace. I had to fully accept that I had nothing to give. All I could do was receive. Sometimes, that's all you can do.

R: And then our daughter was born, and Kristen could breathe normally again. Which was a euphoric moment, to say the least. But what we weren't prepared for were the months following the birth, when Kristen was recovering not just from birth, but from the three months of serious trauma before the birth—like almost drowning for three months, and then making it to shore. You wouldn't order a piña colada and grab a magazine; you'd collapse in a heap on the sand and sob.

K: I had this need to process what had happened and work through it. Rob was endlessly patient, listening to me talk about it over and over.

R: This would often happen when we took walks.

K: It reminds me of the time we rented a moped in Monaco and rode along the French Riviera.

R: It does? What does the moped have to do with the asthma?

K: We had to rent it trying to speak French, which we don't do very well, and we weren't really sure what the driving laws were and we didn't have a map and we didn't know where we were going but the weather was beautiful and we ended up in Eze, this little village above the sea and there was a garden on top of the mountain—it was magical. Marriage includes all of it—the highs and lows, the times when you're in the ER and the times when you're literally on top of a mountain. When I think back to the beginning, I realize that when I got in Rob's truck at LAX, I had no idea where we were going.

R: To my grandma's apartment.

K: Yes, but I'm speaking in a much broader sense about our life together. We had no idea of the vast and varied experiences that we were going to have together.

R: Like raising our kids.

K: Or writing a book.

R: Or when we moved into that condo and they put a cell phone tower up outside the boys' bedroom.

K: Or the times when the kids and I are traveling with Rob when he speaks somewhere, and protestors are in front of the venue holding up signs about how dangerous he is.

It's easy to divide your experiences in marriage into the good ones and the bad ones.

The modern world tends to prefer these sorts of binaries—good *or* bad, success *or* failure, happy *or* sad. Nice, neat either/or categories.

But the longer you're married the more you see that everything that comes your way is an opportunity to find God and each other in new ways. In the asthma, the moped, the trips to Target for trash bags and everything in between, **we are invited to transcend those binaries, becoming aware of the divine presence in all of life.**

|||||||||||||||||||||||||

At first, it was just you, and then you zimzumed, taking a leap, creating space for another to thrive.

Sometimes you have to return to that initial leap, reminding each other of the story that is uniquely and exclusively *your* story.

Sometimes you have to consciously, intentionally throw out the scorecard, deciding together to not let the past shape the future.

Sometimes you have to stop beating yourself up for mistakes you've made, trusting that this other person will give you the divine grace to start again.

And then sometimes it's as simple as doing something really generous and kind for this person you've given yourself to. Unexpected generosity has a way of unleashing new possibilities and invigorating the space between you in significant ways.

We've seen marriages fall apart. We've seen people wound each other in ways that their marriage never recovers from. We've seen marriages where one person is giving it everything they have and the other has given up. We've seen people taking steps to be healthier but they're married to someone who is destructive and has no interest in changing.

We've also seen marriages resurrected. Marriages in which it would take a miracle for the wounds to heal and the love to flow again. But it happened. The old burned to the ground, and in the ashes something new was born.

God is present in the space between you. You are not on your own. When you come to the end of your strength and your ideas and your efforts and your plans, you will be in the place where you receive a new vision for the future.

Marriages, from time to time, need renewal, a fresh start, a new beginning. Whether your marriage appears to be dead, or you simply need a new vision for your life together, few things are more powerful than hope. And hope is divine.

|||||||||||||||||||||||

There are times in marriage for *analyzing*—figuring out how to understand each other better, how to help the other thrive, how to be more intentional about your own health—but your marriage is also a mystery. And mysteries are less about analyzing and more about *enjoying*.

Of the seven billion people on the planet, why this one person? Whatever answer you give, it will be an answer that takes you deeper into the mystery.

Several years ago our next door neighbor Donna came to the end of a long battle with cancer. She was moved to hospice care where Bill, her husband of fifty years, sat by her bed every day. At one point their rabbi visited them, and at the end of the visit he told Bill that it was probably time for Bill to let Donna go.

And so Bill sat down next to the bed and began to talk to her. He told her how much he loved her and how amazing it had been to be with her for all of those years, and then he told her that he sensed this was the end and the best thing for him to do was to let her go.

He finished talking to her, she took a few breaths, and then she stopped breathing.

None of us has any idea what tomorrow will bring, but we found each other, and we get to enjoy today together.

This picture of us was taken in San Diego in the winter of 2003. As you can see, someone took it from behind us as we were walking across the parking lot of a hotel. *We love this picture.* We love it for what it says and what it doesn't say: It's clear we're headed somewhere, but it isn't clear at all where that somewhere is. What is clear is that wherever that somewhere is, we're headed there together.

There was that moment when we first sat in that truck at LAX and realized that fireworks were going off.

R: And I asked, *What percentage of your visit is actually to look for a place to live?*

K: And I said, *It makes a great excuse.*

It was more than a great excuse,
it was the beginning of a zimzum,
a zimzum of love.

QUESTIONS

What's a Zimzum?

What was your center of gravity like when you first met him/her? (Work, school, friends, family, interests, etc.)

How did your center of gravity expand after you met them?

What ways did you create space in your own life so this other person could thrive?

How would you describe the energy flow between the two of you?

Responsive

Everything you say and think and do affects the space between you. How have you seen this at work in your relationship?

What does your partner want out of life?

What does it look like for them to thrive?

What are their hopes and dreams and goals?

Can they name and describe what it looks like for you to thrive? Do you have the sense that they are as committed to your hopes and dreams and goals as you are?

Whatever we put into our relationship is multiplied whether good or bad. Describe a time when the generative nature of the space between you took something small and made it big.

How have you seen the scorecard at work in your relationship?

What do you want for your marriage?

What does your partner want?

What do you both want for your life together?

Dynamic

What have been some of the most recent seasons of your relationship, and how have they been different from one another?

Describe a time your partner surprised you.

What do we mean when we say that you're endlessly *figuring it out* together?

Is there an area of your relationship that you feel you should have figured out by now but you haven't?

Is there an area of your relationship that is taking some time to figure out and over which you might need to relax and give each other grace?

How would you describe the space between you in terms of distance?

Is there anything that's not working for you in the relationship that you've never talked about?

What topics make you most defensive? Why?

What comes to mind when you read *they're like you but not like you*?

What are your triggers?

What are your default patterns when things get tense?

What are topics that you continually argue about? Why those particular topics?

What is the "issue behind the issue"? What does your spouse need to hear from you about that issue?

In what ways do the two of you see the world differently? How has this made you a better person?

What does it mean to gain another set of eyes?

Exclusive

How are you entangled?

Describe the last adventure you had together.

What's in your collective memory that only the two of you share?

How would you describe your own process of leaving and cleaving?

What assumptions did you each bring to your marriage about money, sex, relatives, kids, holidays, work, social obligations?

How is this person "home" for you?

What adventures or new experiences do you have planned?

Describe a time when someone was in the space between you who didn't belong there.

How does having something just between the two of you make your bonds even stronger?

What inside language and jokes do the two of you share?

Sacred

How does your partner accepting you exactly as you are compel you to be a better person?

When have you experienced grace through your spouse? Was it something they said or something they did?

When have you been aware that what was going on between the two of you went *beyond* the two of you?

What does it mean to be fully present in your body?

What does it look like to be comfortable in your own skin?

How is sex spiritual?

How is sex related to grace?

How has this person you love shown you the divine?

Do you need to forgive your partner for anything?

Describe a time when they told you everything is going to be fine and you believed them.

How does fidelity create a place that is whole in a fragmented world?

How have you seen a great marriage spill over into the world around them?

What does it look like for your marriage to have a mission?

ENDNOTES, COMMENTARY,
AND A WORD FROM BOB DYLAN

What's a Zimzum?

The dating site match.com gets around seventeen million unique visitors *a month*. According to findthebest.com.

We met on a tennis court our freshman year.

R: This is probably going to sound a little Jane Austenish, but I have very clear memories of meeting Kristen for the first time because she carried herself with a particular dignity that I found compelling. She was different, but good different. Great different. She had a calm and a stillness about her that fascinated me. It was like a quiet confidence, like she knew who she was and she wasn't looking for a man to give her a sense of worth or value.

K: I had a pastor in high school who talked often about the importance of knowing who you are and not defining yourself by who you are with. He taught about being a whole person in yourself and not getting your worth or identity from dating someone. I even remember him asking once about a boyfriend I had: *Is this the best, or are you settling? Because you're better than that.*

R: Interesting that I picked up on that when I first met her, isn't it?

There is a paradox at the heart of the love:

You don't need anybody,
but you need someone.
You are fine on your own,
but you are not fine on your own.

How many times have you heard a married couple tell how they met and one of them begins with *I wasn't looking for anybody*?

You're whole and you're complete, and you don't *need* anyone, but you also have this sense when you meet this person that you need *them*. That without them you are in some hard-to-explain way *not* complete.

You were fine as just you. You weren't aware that you needed someone, but suddenly you can't imagine living without them.

Imagine there was no chocolate in the world because chocolate didn't exist and no one ever talked about chocolate because such a thing couldn't be conceived. We would be fine and we would have no cravings for chocolate because, after all, what is chocolate? What are you talking about? I have no idea what this chocolate is that you speak of!

Then someone gives you chocolate.

You now have tasted, and this taste has created a hunger for something that you previously had no craving for because you had no idea it even existed. Now you've had chocolate, and you will never be the same.

Rob's band. The band was called Ton Bundle.

A MasterCraft, which to me was the greatest boat a person could own. It was the 1982 Stars and Stripes special addition, and her dad had kept it covered in the garage so it was in perfect condition. Boat nerds loved that last sentence. You know who you are.

I knew what I was getting into, and I'm not just talking about the truck. No matter how long you've known the person or how well you know the person, there's always a risk. How is it that we can put a man on the moon and a thousand songs in our pocket and yet we can't come up with a survey or test or compatibility questionnaire that will guarantee that this person will not break your heart? Love is more mysterious and risky than ever. But if you took the leap, the risk, the chance out of it, it wouldn't be love.

Specifically, to my grandma's apartment.

R: I need to tell at least one story about my grandma because she was a great woman who would once in a while say the strangest things. Her name was Ruth, and she was an art teacher and she was four feet nine inches tall on a good day. One night while I was living with her, I was out in Huntington Beach, driving around in my truck, about to make a left turn. A sixteen-year-old girl was coming the other way with a car full of friends and ran the oncoming red light just as I was turning and hit me head on. Completely totaled that truck. I was fine, but I had to walk for a while to find a place to call a taxi, and I didn't get back to the apartment until late in the night. The next morning I told my grandma about the accident, and her first response was, "You weren't running from the Lord, were you?"

The upside is infinite. Many thanks to Mike McHargue for that line.

The more random the better.

R: Catty Wompus was a band in Chicago around 1990 that my band played shows with—they had a song called "Spork" that contained the fantastic chorus "Spork! It's a spoon and a fork!" Rusty Kleenex was a band I went to high school with. They changed their name from Puddle Slug so that they would, you know, reach more fans. *Engelbert Humperdinck*—Eddie Izzard does a bit about this singer's name in his film *Dress to Kill.* Wait—what? You don't know who Eddie Izzard is? *Unpidgeonholeable.* What can I say about that word that it doesn't say in all its beauty and magnificence? *Fog index* measures how readable a piece of writing is. *The History of Fishes* was a book published by the Royal Society in London in 1686 about, well, the history of fishes. Interestingly enough, the society spent all its money putting the book out and it sold next to no copies, so the society couldn't pay for the publication of another little book of the time by a man named Isaac Newton called *Principia*—which sold a kajillion copies and changed the modern world.

In the last page of the endnotes in his book *What We Talk About When We Talk About God* Rob gives a list of words. They're on page 225.

Zimzum (originally *tzimtzum*) is a Hebrew word used in the rabbinic tradition to talk about the creation of the world. The rabbi most closely associated with zimzum is Isaac Luria, who was born in Jerusalem in 1534.

Responsive

This movement is the foundation of your life together. It can't be stressed enough that it takes two to zimzum. Two arrows, two people each giving for the other.

I'll blame it on being an introvert. Susan Cain has written an excellent book on being an introvert called *Quiet: The Power of Introverts in a World That Can't Stop Talking.* You can see her TED talk at TED.com.

Your emotional health matters. For a great, accessible book on emotional health, see Peter Scazzero's *Emotionally Healthy Spirituality.*

The final season of the television show *Friday Night Lights.*

R: Is this the greatest series ever? Or is it *Lost*? Or *The Wire*? Or *Breaking Bad*? (I can hear someone yelling "Mad Men!" as I write this.) This will be debated for ages, but seriously, when Coach goes to the mall on the way to the game and tells Tami that he wants her to take him with her to Philadelphia—how great is that scene?

They know without a shadow of a doubt that you'd lay down your life for them. It's written in the Gospel of John (15:13), "Greater love has no one than this: to lay down one's life for one's friends."

I am my beloved's and my beloved is mine is from Song of Songs 6:3.

Dynamic

When we started a church.

R: I wrote about starting the church in my first book, *Velvet Elvis.*

You're one—but you're not the same. "We're one but we're not the same" is a line from the U2 song "One" on the *Achtung Baby* album.

God gives grace to the humble. See James 4:6.

Because you have *your* eyes, *your* perspective, *your* way of seeing things. And they have *their* eyes, *their* perspective, *their* way of seeing things. We highly recommend familiarizing yourself with the Enneagram, a way of understanding personality types. It has been one of the most useful tools we've come across to help us understand ourselves and each other. (According to the Enneagram, there are nine main personality types. For the record, Kristen is a 6 and Rob is a 7.) One of the best books about the Enneagram, what it is, and how it works, is Richard Rohr's *The Enneagram*. Or if you'd like to start with a book specifically about how the Enneagram works in marriage, we recommend Jennifer P. Schneider and Ron Corn's book *Understand Yourself, Understand Your Partner: The Essential Enneagram Guide to a Better Relationship*.

Boundaries and budgets. The king of helping people make budgets and get out of debt is a fella named Dave Ramsey who writes books and does seminars. Google him.

From speeding tickets.

K: Rob has been pulled over for speeding at least six times since we've been married. Somehow, he got out of all those tickets.

R: "These are not the droids you're looking for."

K: Is that a *Star Wars* reference to Jedi mind tricks?

R: Yep.

K: But last year in Arizona, after twenty years his mind tricks didn't work. He was pulled over and given a ticket. And he had to go to online traffic school.

The Bible begins with a poem. Genesis 1. For a great perspective on water in the Hebrew scriptures, see Bruce Feiler's book *Walking the Bible: A Journey by Land Through the Five Books of Moses.*

Exclusive

In quantum physics. For an excellent and accessible introduction to quantum physics, see Fred A. Wolf's book *Taking the Quantum Leap: The New Physics for Nonscientists* (HarperCollins, 1989).

From *Science News:* "Entanglement is one of the weirdest features of quantum physics. It refers to a situation in which two 'particles' (a term that must be construed loosely in the quantum world) share a common history that makes their futures intertwined." https://www.sciencenews.org/blog/context/einstein -was-wrong-about-spooky-quantum-entanglement.

Years ago we went on a trip with a couple . . .

There is reconciled humor, and then there is unreconciled humor. We all have quirks and funny habits and things we do that make no sense. That's part of being a living, breathing human. When you and your spouse can laugh about your odd habits or stupid jokes, it's endearing. It brings you together. It bonds you. It's not a source of tension or strife; it's shared enjoyment. You've made peace with it. Unreconciled humor is when you see someone laughing at something that they haven't made peace with about their spouse. They laugh not in an endearing way, but to relieve the tension of whatever it is the two of them haven't resolved.

A man will leave his father and mother. Genesis 2:24.

Sacred

Someone who would rub their back while they threw up. From the book *Mating Intelligence Unleashed: The Role of the Mind in Sex, Dating, and Love,* by Glenn Geher and Scott Barry Kaufman (Oxford, 2013), cited in *Elle* magazine (February 2013, p. 142).

Grace and truth meeting together. Psalm 85:10.

Grace is sacred and so is forgiveness. Forgiving doesn't always mean forgetting. In the most ideal situations, it does mean forgetting, but sometimes you forgive and you *remember.* You set up boundaries. You get help. You don't put yourself in a situation to be hurt like that again.

God is love. 1 John 4:8.

Love covers over a multitude of sins. 1 Peter 4:8.

Trinity. Or tri-unity. Often referred to as Father, Son, and Holy Spirit.

A Few More Words from Kristen

Celebrate your anniversary by going somewhere together.

Some years this may mean a week together somewhere you've always wanted to go. Other years it may mean staying in a hotel for a night just down the street. Even if you have to borrow a tent or sleep in your car, it's significant to get away just the two of you to remember why you got married, reflect on this life you are creating together, and mark the occasion of being married another year. I was recently talking to a couple who have taken some sort of anniversary trip every year for forty years. They were attempting to recall all the places they have been together to celebrate and you could tell that this shared history was a source of great joy and meaning.

Remember the story of how you met.

It brings you back to that powerful impulse you had in the beginning where you would do anything for this person that you love. It helps you see them in a fresh light. It reminds you of the incredible thing that the two of you share.

"So how did you meet?" is a great question to ask other couples. It's amazing how much you learn about people when you hear their story.

Be careful of your expectations.

Find your happiness within yourself, not in someone else. If you expect the person you married to make you happy it will kill your relationship and leave you endlessly frustrated and angry. The two of you are figuring it out together, both marriage and life.

Try to go to bed at the same time and always say good night.

A Few More Words from Rob

There's magic in the details. Flowers are gold, and so is cooking. Handwritten notes are spectacular.

A man named Qoos (pronounced "Kwiss") once told me that when a woman is loved well, she opens up like a flower. Ponder this, my young Padawan, and then take appropriate action.

A friend of mine was recently telling me about his father, who is a doctor and saved up a fair bit of money over the years. A little while ago his wife, my friend's mother, died, and you know what he told my friend his one regret in life is? That he didn't spend more money on his wife.

Don't say *"my* house" or "*I* bought it" or "*I'm* thinking about going to Ohio" if the two of you own the house and the two of you bought it and the two of you are going to Ohio. You're in this together, and the pronouns you use are a big deal. *WE.*

You know that dude who won't take dance classes with his wife even though she keeps asking him to? Dude is missing out. If she wants to go somewhere or do something or try something new or step out, do it.

There are moments when I'm reading and I come across something that makes me want to stand up and cheer. This is one of those passages. I suggest memorizing it and then busting it out on the proper occasion, with conviction and passion, even if you don't know what it means. It's from the great theologian Jürgen Moltmann, and it's awesome. Enjoy:

> **Lovers experience each other as counterpart and**
> **presence. Their subjectivity becomes soluble in their**

relationships and concentrates itself once again in their own individual being, and it is in this rhythm that their intersubjective shared life emerges in mutual love as they arrive at one another and themselves. They mutually come close to one another and to themselves. These experiences of personhood are different from the experiences of the solitary object acting on objects; in the flow between counterpart and presence, a personhood comes into being with permeable frontiers, in energy charged relationships. Selfhood is not arrived at by way of demarcations and differentiations. it comes to its full flowering through the power of life-giving relationships. *(The Spirit of Life, p. 287)*

One last word about marriage from Bob Dylan.

From an interview with *Rolling Stone* magazine, September 27, 2012:

RS: What's your estimation of President Obama been when you've met him?

Bob Dylan: What do I think of him? I like him. But you're asking the wrong person. You know who you should be asking that to? You should be asking his wife what she thinks of him. She's the only one that matters.

THANKS

A thousand thanks to . . .

Mickey Maudlin for the editing, guidance, wisdom, and support.

All the great people at HarperOne: Mark Tauber, Claudia Boutote, Katy Hamilton, Suzanne Wickham, Michele Wetherbee, Laina Adler, Terri Leonard, Kim Dayman.

Carlton Cuse for the insightful notes.

Mike McHargue for the illuminating morning discussing the physics of the heart.

Lisa Zuniga for great editing work once again.

Chris Ferebee for reading draft after draft, helping get us unstuck, giving great perspective, and always being a friend.

WILLIAM
COLLINS